# The Religious Rhetoric of U.S. Presidential Candidates

I0129107

Drawing on corpus linguistic methods of analysis, this book critically examines the "rhetorical God gap" in American political discourse between the Democratic and Republican parties. The volume investigates the claims (which have often not been substantiated by quantitative data in the literature and have tended to focus on particular genres of political discourse) that there is a correlation between a higher degree of religiosity in Republican political discourse and voting preferences for the party and that Democratic politicians should engage in similar discourse toward "closing" the gap. The book adopts a keyword approach, using such techniques as collocation analyses, concordance reading, and Bible-specific N-gram identification, toward the study of a corpus of general campaign speeches over a 50-year period, and links findings from this data with social and cultural contextual factors to provide a more informed understanding of rhetorical patterns in religiously laden political language. The volume showcases the value of corpus linguistic methods in interrogating claims around political language and their broader applicability in linguistic research, making this key reading for students and scholars in corpus linguistics, critical discourse analysis, American politics, and religious studies.

**Arnaud Vincent** is an invited professor of linguistics at the Université Saint-Louis—Bruxelles and scientific collaborator at the Centre for English Corpus Linguistics, Université Catholique de Louvain, Belgium. He holds a master's degree in American studies from Antwerp University and a PhD in linguistics from the Université Catholique de Louvain.

## Routledge Advances in Corpus Linguistics
Edited by Tony McEnery
*Lancaster University, UK*

### Michael Hoey
*Liverpool University, UK*

For more information about this series, please visit: https://www.routledge.com/Routledge-Advances-in-Corpus-Linguistics/book-series/SE0593

# The Religious Rhetoric of U.S. Presidential Candidates

A Corpus Linguistics Approach to the Rhetorical God Gap

**Arnaud Vincent**

Routledge
Taylor & Francis Group

LONDON AND NEW YORK

First published 2020 by Routledge

2 Park Square, Milton Park, Abingdon, Oxon, OX14 4RN
605 Third Avenue, New York, NY 10017

*Routledge is an imprint of the Taylor & Francis Group, an informa business*

First issued in paperback 2020

*Library of Congress Cataloging-in-Publication Data*
A catalog record for this book has been requested

ISBN: 978-0-367-14126-4 (hbk)
ISBN: 978-0-367-78778-3 (pbk)

Typeset in Times New Roman
by Apex CoVantage, LLC.

To Jack and Fanny, for being the best teachers ever
To Julie, Héloïse and Lucie, with all my love

# Contents

# Figures

# Tables

# Acknowledgements

Writing this book has been the final step of a very long journey which I certainly did not plan to embark on a few years ago. It is because several people believed in me more than I ever did myself that I eventually undertook it and ventured into territories that I thought were not accessible to me. "We all make history in our own ways". This is what Professor John Alonzo Dick—or Jack as he likes to be called—wrote to me once. I do not know how much history I have made so far—probably very little—but I know for certain that Jack has played a major role in my own history. As a professor of American studies, he was the one who introduced me to the American way of religion. He was also the first person to nudge me into undertaking a PhD research on politics and religion and accompanied me during the entire process. I will be forever grateful to him for leading me in that direction. I voluntarily refrained from talking about the book with Jack—although his insights would undoubtedly have enriched it—as I wanted it to be a surprise for him and a tribute to all he has done for me. Jack is one of the persons to whom I would like to dedicate this book.

I will also be forever grateful to Professor Fanny Meunier who served as my PhD advisor with true kindness, good humour, great wit and a never fading trust in my ability. Although I defended my thesis back in 2014, Fanny has always been there for me ever since, including for the present book. I have lost count of all the ways I am indebted to Fanny, but Fanny does not keep count. She supports her students and colleagues and helps them become better versions of themselves. She truly is one of the best teachers and colleagues I have been fortunate to work with. I want to dedicate the book to her too.

I would like to extend my deepest gratitude to Professor Tony McEnery, first for serving as a member of my PhD jury, then for inviting me to Lancaster University to present my research, and—above all—for believing in me and nudging me into writing the present book while at a conference in Sienna. Never would I have considered working on such a project if it had not been for Tony's encouragements.

xiv  *Acknowledgements*

I am grateful to Professor Michael Hoey for his generosity in providing insightful feedback on a very short notice. Of course, all remaining mistakes are mine alone.

I feel very fortunate to have this book published by Routledge. I want to thank Elysse Preposi, Alexandra Simmons, Helena Parkinson and Autumn Spalding for guiding me through the many steps that publishing involves. I am also grateful to the two anonymous reviewers for their insightful comments.

Most important of all, I want to dedicate the book to my wife Julie and my two daughters Héloïse and Lucie. Julie has accompanied me to conferences, read countless drafts and always offered an attentive ear to my never-ending doubts, all in the midst of her wonderfully successful career and a happy—but really busy—family life. It is no exaggeration to say that Julie has been our family's rock, and I feel so fortunate to have met her and married her. To Lucie and Héloïse I owe countless hugs, games not yet played, fun still to be had, and probably some less daddy-friendly activities too (doing nails is not an option though). In spite of all these missed opportunities, they have remained wonderfully patient and understanding. Most of all, they have brought us joy and true meaning in our lives.

# Introduction

Thus far, the existence of a gap separating the religious rhetoric of the American Republican Party from that produced by the Democratic Party has largely been taken as an article of faith derived from the so-called "God gap theory", which posits that a higher degree of religiosity correlates with a higher voting preference for the Republican Party (Smidt et al. 2010: 3). Two premises traditionally accompany this alleged difference (hencefor-ward called the "rhetorical God gap")[1] in the religious language produced by each party. According to the first premise, the Republicans have played the religious rhetoric card with much more intensity and skill than their Democratic Party counterparts. This belief in the Republicans' skilful and more intense exploitation of religious language is reinforced by the sec-ond premise, which holds that religious rhetoric actually matters, notably because it can influence the way people cast their votes and because it will appeal to the "more" (read conservative-style) religious constituencies, which are traditionally described as being both influential and well organ-ized. Put together, these beliefs and assumptions have converged towards the same eureka conclusion: for the Democrats to gain votes among religious people and therefore close the God gap, they have no choice but to engage in more and better religious rhetoric and close the "rhetorical God gap". This conclusion has been widely accepted without seeing its underlying premises much questioned. Indeed, the impact that religious messages may have on the audience remains deeply unclear, one reason being that much of the literature around presidential rhetoric is pervaded by an endemic lack of evidence, notably as regards its effects on the audience (Edwards 2003, 2004). Likewise, no study has yet gathered solid evidence proving the existence of consistent, party-specific linguistic differences that would confirm a skilful and more intense exploitation of religious language by the GOP. One reason for this lies in the fact that most studies conducted so far have taken a rather traditional course where the focus is laid on a limited set of speeches, such as Inaugural speeches, State of the Union addresses, or else so-called "major presidential speeches". In addition to belonging to the same presidential rhetoric category, some among these speeches are so much constrained by genre-specific features that generalizations going beyond these very specific genres seem dubious at best, yet the literature is ripe with such generalizations. That such a methodological course has been the preferred option for studying the use of religious language in American politics is difficult to reconcile with the fact that this use is widely alleged to serve the electoral process and—so goes the belief—help the candidates gain votes. The modern U.S. presidency is commonly described as evolving in a permanent campaign context, which is said to blur the lines separating the time in office and the time on the campaign trail. There may thus be some validity in the study of presidential language to get a better sense of how religion can be exploited for electoral gain. Yet, when it comes to the understanding of the exploitation of religion for the very purpose of winning elections, it seems important—although still not enough—to study the religiously laden language produced by presidential candidates themselves. Truistic as this may sound—and in spite of the strong confidence accompanying many claims on the use of religious language in the electoral process—such studies have remained mostly absent from the literature. True, several scholars have brought some interesting insights or even quantitative (albeit often debatable) evidence to either the study of American political language (e.g. Hart et al. 2005), the study of presidential rhetoric and campaign rhetoric (e.g. Hart 2002; Hart and Childers 2005; Jarvis 2005; Lim 2008), or—to come closer to our own field of interest—the study of religious language in presidential campaigns and/or presidential rhetoric (e.g. Chapp 2007, 2009, 2012; Domke and Coe 2008; Kaylor 2010, 2011; Kradel 2004, 2008, 2009; Schonhardt-Bailey et al. 2012; Stecker 2011; Warber and Olson 2007; Weiss (ed.) 2010). However, many among those studies still rely on very specific case studies, unrepresentative samples of political religious language, and/or arbitrarily chosen words and untested premises which serve to launch top-down investigations.

The present research seeks to address these shortcomings by adopting an approach where corpus linguistic methods are used—mostly in a bottom-up corpus-driven fashion (Tognini-Bonelli 2001)—to track down linguistic traces of this alleged—but still unproven and unmeasured—rhetorical God gap. The primary source for this investigation is a corpus of general election campaign speeches produced by both parties from 1952 to 2008 (2890 speeches; 6.1 million words). When needed, the data extracted from this main source are further enriched by explorations into other specialized corpora, to wit, a corpus of presidential rhetoric (1789–2009, 59.7 million words), Domke and Coe's 1933–2007 corpus of major presidential speeches (Domke and Coe 2008, 1 million words), a corpus of campaign ads (1952–1996, 153,618 words), and a corpus of National Party Platforms (1900–2008, 764,110 words). A corpus containing all the primary debates held in the 2016 presidential campaign (513,646 words, GOP and Democratic Party) and a corpus of Christian hymns (242 hymns, 32,994 words) came as two late additions to these corpora and were explored while writing Chapter 3 and 4 of the present book. An electronic version of the King James Bible was also part of the sources we exploited to find evidence for the rhetorical God gap.

Specifically, the book explores and discusses several patterns of religious language that were extracted via a "key keyword" approach (Scott 2008) and further analyzed with techniques such as collocation analyses, keyword analyses, concordance reading and Bible-specific N-gram identification. In the present study, efforts are also made to reconnect the results with their contextual factors and illuminate them with insights borrowed from the American studies tradition. In triangulating the approaches to the rhetorical God gap, the present study therefore frees itself from the narrow confines of a single discipline or from the commonly adopted case-study approach tradition and offers instead the possibility of observing the data from a range of complementary perspectives. Through a combination of bottom-up, top-down, quantitative, qualitative, macroscopic, microscopic, diachronic and synchronic analyses, this study unearths a variety of patterns of religiously laden language, which altogether combine into a patchwork of party-, time- and/or candidate-specific rhetorical features. The resulting picture challenges the simplistic belief in a monolithic rhetorical gap separating an all religious GOP from a religiously voiceless Democratic Party. Likewise, the present study provides evidence against some all-the-rage—but wrong—theories presenting today's rhetorical usages of religion in American politics as unprecedented. Not only does the corpus linguistic approach help get a richer and more nuanced depiction of the religious rhetoric employed by U.S. presidential candidates, but it also returns some highly counterintuitive findings. The recurring presence of biblical language—from single word-units to larger verbatim quotes from the Bible and Christian hymns—almost exclusively in the Democratic Party camp is a case in point.

Although the present book is not methodological in nature—discussions over corpora and methods will be kept to a minimum to leave room for the presentation and interpretation of results—it can be viewed as methodological in purpose since one of its aims is to demonstrate how tried and tested corpus linguistic techniques and the triangulation of different perspectives can help address some of the shortcomings of the current literature. Likewise, this research is driven by the desire to answer the call for different disciplines to enter the game and study religious rhetoric in such a way as to identify patterns of language that go beyond mere isolated cases (Warber and Olson 2007: 1–4) and which are supported by evidence rather than by arguments and intuitions alone. By reviewing—sometimes at length—some of the claims made in the literature, this study aims to illustrate why these claims are problematic, how corpus linguistic methods can help address them and why better research practices should be developed in the future. Otherwise stated, the present book aims to serve as an echo chamber to the calls long made for better ways of approaching political language (see for e.g. King 1993; Edwards 2003, 2004) and as a demonstration of how corpus linguistics can help get a richer and more accurate picture of a phenomenon that is still in need of more research.

## Summary of Chapters

Chapter 1 lays the necessary methodological groundwork by providing a condensed description of the methods and the corpora used for the present research. It also reviews some of the main limitations thereof. As said above, the methodological descriptions will be kept to a minimum as the methods used do not really break any methodological ground. Such methods—and the specific use of them for the study of political language—have been amply described and discussed in former seminal work (e.g. Baker 2006, 2009; Baker et al. 2008; McEnery et al. 2006; Morley and Bayley (eds.) 2013; Partington 2003; Partington et al. 2013). The remainder of the book will be articulated around three main types of findings, each type corresponding to one chapter. The first type (Chapter 2) concerns findings that are illustrative of the religiously laden language produced during the Cold War era and driven by that very historical context more than by party-specific proclivities. The resulting trend presented in Chapter 2 is therefore not so much representative of a party as it is of an era. The next two chapters (**Chapters 3** and **4**) both present findings which can be viewed as party specific, although this categorization does not imply that such party-specific trends are not impacted by variables other than the political parties they are said to represent. More specifically, Chapter 3 accounts for GOP-specific religious language, while Chapter 4 focuses on the religiously laden items that characterize the Democratic Party speeches. A more detailed description of chapters 2, 3 and 4 follows.

### *Chapter 2*

Chapter 2 provides a condensed account of several linguistic traces of cold-war-specific religious language. The "gap" thus discovered does not so much cut through party lines as through time as it isolates the Cold War rhetoric from other eras and shows how specific such rhetoric is in its exploitation—by both parties—of a religiously laden rhetorical arsenal against godless Communism. Although primarily time-specific, this Cold War religious rhetoric is further explored in Chapter 2 for potential traces of party- and/or candidate-specific features. Whilst a few traces of more idiosyncratic features are discovered and further discussed, the main conclusion of Chapter 2 is that of a religiously laden language used by both parties as an ecumenical call of sorts to fight against godless Communism. This Cold War religious rhetoric is further discussed in Chapter 2 for what it can bring to our understanding of more recent trends. More specifically, it helps call into question the way some media outlets interpreted the language that George W. Bush had used to sell the US-led "war on terror". Likewise, the analyses conducted on the religiously laden Cold War rhetoric serve to qualify the depiction by scholarly work of the term *crusade* as the product of a fairly modern electoral strategy and a term mostly representative of George W. Bush's rhetoric.

## *Chapter 3*

Chapter 3 helps answer the question, *which specific features are most characteristic of the religious language produced by the GOP?* More specifically, it gives an account of several patterns of language that are mostly salient in the rhetoric produced by GOP candidates from the late 1970s onwards and which are linked to the religiously laden culture war issues of abortion, gay marriage, family values, stem cell research and judicial activism. Chapter 3 briefly explains how these culture war issues are linked to the intricate entanglement of politics and religion in the U.S. and why the language that is salient in the GOP camp can be viewed as religiously laden and therefore relevant to our quest for the rhetorical God gap. The location of these several patterns of language on party and time lines and their links with these culture war issues appear quite in sync with the traditional depiction of the GOP's usage of religious language and the subsequent conventional understanding of the rhetorical God gap. While the present study demonstrates how limited such understanding can be when compared to the richer reality it unearths, Chapter 3 provides quantitative evidence that nonetheless supports some of its tenets and in turn confirms that there is some validity—although limited—to it. By extracting and exploring data from different corpora, Chapter 3 also complements previous scholarly work on the rhetoric around these culture war issues.

Still in Chapter 3, the notion of "issue ownership" (see for example Damore 2004, 2005; Doherty 2008; Kaufmann 2004) is discussed while trying to reconcile (1) the relatively equal measure of references to "family values" in the rhetoric of both parties with (2) the consensual understanding—even conceded by Democratic Party candidates themselves—that the GOP owns these so-called family values. One important message of Chapter 3 is therefore that differences separating the GOP from the Democratic Party can materialize elsewhere than in mere quantitative differences.

Finally, Chapter 3 contains an analysis of the evolution of the term *liberal*. More specifically, it confirms previous scholarly observations (see for example Jarvis 2005, Nunberg 2006) and demonstrates (both quantitatively and qualitatively) how this term—once proudly endorsed by Democratic Party candidates—left the Democratic Party rhetoric while being recuperated by 1980s-onwards GOP candidates who have since turned it into a bad word to accuse "the liberals"—i.e. the Democrats—of several culture-war-related charges. Now in the mouth of GOP candidates, the term *liberal* is equated with being unfriendly towards religion and therefore on the fringe of being un-American, as well as with being socialist, pro-gay, pro-abortion, soft on foreign political issues, elitist, pro big government, pro Hollywood and disconnected with true (read conservative) Americans. This displacement of the term *liberal* from the older Democratic Party's rhetoric to the 1980s-onwards GOP's language is all the more interesting as it seems to parallel a modification in the paradigm used to describe the American religious landscape and the different groups forming it. According to this new paradigm, what unites or else separates religious groups from one another is not so much defined by their faith traditions as it is by their respective position on a conservative-progressive line defining their religious behaviour. In other words, understanding the American religious landscape would now require taking into consideration what position people adopt on this liberal-conservative spectrum along with more traditional variables like the religious tradition one belongs to. Chapter 3 discusses the modifications that the term *liberal* has undergone in campaign rhetoric in the light of this new framework.

## Chapter 4

Chapter 4 focuses on three main findings that help describe the religious language produced by the Democratic Party. In doing so, Chapter 4 aims to answer a question that is similar to that posed in Chapter 3, but which centres around the Democratic Party language instead. First, the salient and somehow persistent usage of the term *catholic* is discussed and further analyzed. Secondly, the "brotherhood" rhetoric that is also salient in the Democratic Party camp is detailed and linked to the notion of "religious left". Last but certainly not least, Chapter 4 describes the unprecedented and quite unexpected discovery of a "Bible pattern"—made of direct references to the Bible and verbatim quotes from it—which marks the Democratic Party rhetoric. Based on this discovery, an in-depth discussion of Berlinerblau's book (2008) on the use of the Bible in politics is conducted. The purpose is not to attack Berlinerblau or criticize his work just for the sake of it. Rather, this discussion aims to illustrate why King's advice towards scholars of rhetoric—"It takes much more than a cogently argued point to verify an empirical claim about the world" (1993: 391)—needs to be heard once and for all and why failing to take such advice has led even the most knowledge-able scholars on the wrong track.

## Note

1. Kaylor (2010) used the term "rhetorical God gap" in a 2010 paper on the 2004 religious-political rhetoric of George W. Bush and John F. Kerry. If anything, Kaylor's paper is mostly an invitation to study what he labels "the rhetorical God gap". The fact that we use this very label constitutes an acknowledgment of sorts to Kaylor's invitation, although the present research question was devised before coming across Kaylor's 2010 paper, and therefore not developed because of it. Also, it is quite doubtful that Kaylor would be willing to claim paternity for such a term, as it must be understood as just another variation of the broader "gapology" literature (Olson and Green 2009: 1–9).

## References

Baker, P. 2006. *Using Corpora in Discourse Analysis*. London: Continuum.
Baker, P. 2009. 'The question is, how cruel is it?' Keywords, Fox Hunting and the House of Commons. In Archer, D. (ed.). *What's in a Word-List? Investigating Word Frequency and Keyword Extraction*. Farnham: Ashgate Publishing Limited, 125–136.
Baker, P., Costas, G., KhosraviNik, M., Krzyzanowski, M., McEnery, T. and Wodak, R. 2008. A Useful Methodological Synergy? Combining Critical Discourse Analysis and Corpus Linguistics to Examine Discourses of Refugees and Asylum Seekers in the UK Press. *Discourse & Society*, Vol. 19, No. 3, 273–306.
Berlinerblau, J. 2008. *Thumpin' It: The Use and Abuse of the Bible in Today's Presidential Politics*. Louisville, KY: Westminster John Knox Press.
Chapp, C. B. 2007. *Religious Campaign Rhetoric: The Consequences of Religious Language on Presidential Candidate Evaluations*. Paper prepared for presentation at the annual meeting of the American Political Science Association, Chicago, IL, August 30, September 2.
Chapp, C. B. 2009. *Religious Political Participation: Affect, Identity, and Rhetorical Cues*. Paper prepared for presentation at the annual meeting of the Midwest Political Science Association, Chicago, IL, April 2–5.
Chapp, C. B. 2012. *Religious Rhetoric and American Politics: The Endurance of Civil Religion in Electoral Campaigns*. Ithaca, NY: Cornell University Press.
Damore, D. F. 2004. The Dynamics of Issue Ownership in Presidential Campaigns. *Political Research Quarterly*, Vol. 57, No. 3 (September), 391–397.
Damore, D. F. 2005. Issue Convergence in Presidential Campaigns. *Political Behavior*, Vol. 27, No. 1 (March), 71–97.
Doherty, D. 2008. Presidential Rhetoric, Candidate Evaluations, and Party Identification: Can Parties "Own" Values? *Political Research Quarterly*, Vol. 61, No. 3 (September), 419–433.
Domke, D. and Coe, K. 2008. *The God Strategy: How Religion Became a Political Weapon in America*. New York: Oxford University Press.

Edwards, G. C. III. 2003. *On Deaf Ears: The Limits of the Bully Pulpit*. New Haven, CT: Yale University Press.

Edwards, G. C. III. 2004. Presidential Rhetoric: What Difference Does It Make? In Medhurst, M. J. (ed.). *Beyond the Rhetorical Presidency* (2nd printing). College Station, TX: Texas A&M University Press, 199–217.

Hart, R. P. 2002. *Campaign Talk: Why Elections Are Good for Us*. Princeton, NJ: Princeton University Press.

Hart, R. P. and Childers, J. P. 2005. The Evolution of Candidate Bush. *American Behavioral Scientist*, Vol. 49, No. 2 (October), 180–197.

Hart, R. P., Jarvis, S. E., Jennings, W. P. and Smith-Howell, D. 2005. *Political Keywords: Using Language that Uses Us*. New York: Oxford University Press.

Jarvis, S. E. 2005. *The Talk of the Party: Political Labels, Symbolic Capital, and American Life*. Lanham, MD: Rowman & Littlefield Publishers, Inc.

Kaufmann, K. M. 2004. Disaggregating and Reexamining Issue Ownership and Voter Choice. *Polity*, Vol. 36, No. 2 (January), 283–299.

Kaylor, B. 2010. A Rhetorical "God Gap": Religious-Political Rhetoric of George W. Bush and John F. Kerry. *Journal of the Speech and Theatre Association of Missouri*, Vol. 40 (Fall), 27–47. http://speechandtheatremo.org/past-journals/ Last consulted: May 23, 2014.

Kaylor, B. 2011. *Presidential Campaign Rhetoric in an Age of Confessional Politics*. Lanham, MD: Lexington Books.

King, G. 1993. The Methodology of Presidential Research. In Edwards, G. C. III., Rockman B. A. and Kessel, J. H. (eds.) *Researching the Presidency: Vital Questions, New Approaches*. Pittsburgh, PA: University of Pittsburgh, 387–412.

Kradel, A. 2004. *God on Our Side: The Religious Rhetoric of Recent U.S. Presidents*. Paper presented at the annual meeting of the American Political Science Association, Hilton Chicago and the Palmer House Hilton, Chicago, IL, September 2.

Kradel, A. 2008. *Using the Lord's Name: The Use and Impact of Presidential Religious Rhetoric*. PhD dissertation. ProQuest: University of Wisconsin-Madison.

Kradel, A. 2009. *What Influences Presidents to Use Religious Rhetoric?* Paper prepared for the 2009 annual meeting of the Midwest Political Science Association, March 30.

Lim, E. T. 2008. *The Anti-Intellectual Presidency: The Decline of Presidential Rhetoric from George Washington to George W. Bush*. New York: Oxford University Press.

McEnery, T., Xiao, R. and Tono, Y. 2006. *Corpus-Based Language Studies: An Advanced Resource Book*. Abingdon, Oxon: Routledge.

Morley, J. and Bayley, P. (eds.). 2013. *Corpus-Assisted Discourse Studies on the Iraq Conflict: Wording the War*. Abingdon, Oxon: Routledge.

Nunberg, G. 2006. *Talking Right: How Conservatives Turned Liberalism into a Tax-Raising, Latte-Drinking, Sushi-Eating, Volvo-Driving, New York Times-Reading, Body-Piercing, Hollywood-Loving, Left-Wing Freak Show*. New York: Public Affairs.

Olson, L. R. and Green, J. C. 2009. "Gapology" and the 2004 Presidential Vote. In Olson, L. R. and Green, J. C. (eds.). *Beyond Red State, Blue State: Electoral Gaps in the Twenty-First Century American Electorate*. Upper Saddle River, NJ: Pearson Prentice Hall, 1–9.

Partington, A. 2003. *The Linguistics of Political Argument: The Spin-Doctor and the Wolf-Pack at the White House*. Abingdon, Oxon: Routledge.

Partington, A, Duguid, A. and Taylor, C. 2013. *Patterns and Meanings in Discourse: Theory and Practice in Corpus-Assisted Discourse Studies (CADS)*. Amsterdam: John Benjamins.

Schonhardt-Bailey, C., Yager, E. and Lahlou, S. 2012. Yes, Ronald Reagan's Rhetoric was Unique—But Statistically, *How* Unique? *Presidential Studies Quarterly*, Vol. 42, No. 3 (September), 482–513.

Scott, M. 2008. *Word Smith Tools* (Version 5). Liverpool: Lexical Analysis Software.

Smidt, C. E., den Dulk, K. R., Froehle, B. T., Penning, J. M., Monsma, S. V. and Koopman, D. L. 2010. *The Disappearing God Gap? Religion in the 2008 Presidential Election*. New York: Oxford University Press.

Stecker, F. 2011. *The Podium, The Pulpit, and the Republicans: How Presidential Candidates Use Religious Language in American Political Debates*. Santa Barbara, CA: Praeger.

Tognini-Bonelli, E. 2001. *Corpus Linguistics at Work*. Amsterdam: John Benjamins.

Warber, A. L. and Olson, L. R. 2007. *Religion and Ronald Reagan's Rhetorical Presidency*. Paper presented at the annual meeting of the American Political Science Association, Hyatt Regency Chicago and the Sheraton Chicago Hotel and Towers, Chicago, IL, August 30.

Weiss, D. (ed.). 2010. *What Democrats Talk about When They Talk about God: Religious Communication in Democratic Party Politics*. Lanham, MD: Lexington Books.

# 1  Methodology and Limitations

## 1.1. Methodology

As explained in the introduction, this study aims to depart from a well-established research tradition in the field of political and religious rhetoric and embark instead on a corpus-assisted exploration of the rhetorical God gap. When sailing into uncharted waters, one should make sure to set the course on some very precise objectives lest one gets lost in the process. For the present study, the following objectives—presented here in the form of "methodological commandments"—served as a compass to decide upon the methods to use and the directions to follow:

(1)  Avoid starting your exploration from preconceived assumptions as to which era or which side of the religious-cum-political spectrum uses religious rhetoric most saliently or skilfully;

(2)  Put each and every presidential candidate on equal footing rather than choose (or cherry-pick) the favourite ones, the most fashionable ones or those who seem to offer the most promising outcomes;

(3)  Find a methodology that helps analyze similarities AND differences between the candidates and eras;

(4)  Do not reduce the rhetorical God gap to a precise set of arbitrarily chosen items to query and analyze (e.g. queries *god/bless/pray/jesus/almighty*);

(5)  Let the data speak first rather than muzzle it with top-down premises and preconceived intuitions. Hypothesis-driven studies and top-down investigations are important, but they come next in methodological order;

(6)  Make room for both quantitative and qualitative investigations;

(7)  Do not forget contextual factors as likely variables to explain what is observed.

The patterns of religiously laden language that are presented in this book were identified through what is known in corpus linguistics as a "key keyword analysis" of a rather extensive computer readable collection—or "corpus"— of presidential general election speeches spanning from 1952 to 2008. The suite of tools used to conduct this key keyword analysis—which is described at greater length below—is Mike Scott's *WordSmith* (version 5.0; Scott 2008).

Tables 1.1 and 1.2 provide statistical details for this 1952–2008 Presidential Campaign Speeches corpus (henceforth referred to as the PCS corpus).

As is apparent from Tables 1.1 and 1.2, there is no file for 2000 as no comprehensive collection for that particular year has been identified so far. The extent to which this absence constitutes a limitation will not be discussed here. However, it seems fair to say that the 2000 campaign files would have been a valuable addition—all the more so when focusing on candidate-specific trends—but would probably not have radically changed the main findings reported in the present book.

As regards the sources exploited to build this 1952–2008 PCS corpus, four can be cited:

- The Annenberg/Pew Archive of Presidential Campaign Discourse for the 1952–1996 campaigns (Kanda Software 2000).
- Woolley and Peters's *The American Presidency Project* website for the 2008 campaign (for both Obama and McCain).
- As regards the 2004 campaign, two sources were exploited. The campaign speeches provided on Medhurst and Stob's *presidentialrhetoric.com* website[1] were used. This collection was complemented with 2004 campaign speeches retrieved from the CORPS corpus (Guerini et al. 2008).

*Table 1.1* Statistics for the Democratic Party Files of the PCS Corpus

| Year | Candidate | N Speeches | Word Size |
|------|-----------|-----------|-----------|
| 1952 | Stevenson | 186 | 331,924 |
| 1956 | Stevenson | 75 | 149,483 |
| 1960 | Kennedy | 312 | 408,395 |
| 1964 | Johnson | 111 | 250,947 |
| 1968 | Humphrey | 153 | 442,530 |
| 1972 | McGovern | 98 | 164,279 |
| 1976 | Carter | 55 | 113,652 |
| 1980 | Carter | 89 | 197,138 |
| 1984 | Mondale | 66 | 119,062 |
| 1988 | Dukakis | 66 | 104,325 |
| 1992 | Clinton | 76 | 234,401 |
| 1996 | Clinton | 111 | 348,854 |
| 2000 | – | – | – |
| 2004 | Kerry | 58 | 143,443 |
| 2008 | Obama | 176 | 468,841 |
| **Total** | | **1632** | **3,477,274** |

*Table 1.2* Statistics for the Republican Party Files of the PCS Corpus

| Year | Candidate | N Speeches | Word Size |
|------|-----------|-----------|-----------|
| 1952 | Eisenhower | 230 | 360,532 |
| 1956 | Eisenhower | 43 | 71,612 |
| 1960 | Nixon | 136 | 410,816 |
| 1964 | – | – | – |
| 1968 | Nixon | 58 | 206,172 |
| 1972 | Nixon | 59 | 112,782 |
| 1976 | Ford | 128 | 148,577 |
| 1980 | Reagan | 69 | 91,109 |
| 1984 | Reagan | 108 | 241,285 |
| 1988 | Bush | 41 | 86,675 |
| 1992 | Bush | 126 | 276,280 |
| 1996 | Dole | 78 | 192,396 |
| 2000 | – | – | – |
| 2004 | Bush | 39 | 182,312 |
| 2008 | McCain | 143 | 277,088 |
| **Total** | | **1258** | **2,657,636** |

Most of the results presented in the this book were extracted via one specific sub-category of a procedure called "keyness analysis". A keyness analysis is a statistical procedure that extracts—from one study corpus file—items that are significantly more frequent (in terms of normalized frequency values) than in a reference norm. The elements that are extracted are called "key" not because of their meaning or the value they may have in the eyes of the analyst. They are defined as "key" by statistical tests, irrespective of the subjective importance one is willing to attribute to them. The WordSmith *KeyWords* tool calculates an objective statistical value—called "keyness value"—for each extracted item. This keyness value corresponds to a statistical score that measures the extent to which a given item departs (in relative frequency) from the reference corpus. The higher the keyness value, the more significant the difference is from the norm.

In this research project, the keyness analysis was used at the word-unit level only, hence its being referred to as a "keyword" analysis. In order to run a keyword analysis with *KeyWords*, two frequency word lists must first be computed via the program *WordList*: one frequency list for the study corpus file, and one frequency list for the reference corpus file. *KeyWords* then compares the study corpus frequency list against the reference corpus frequency list and returns—from the study corpus—a list of statistically significant keywords.

Further, the choice was made to split the collection of campaign speeches along two combined criteria, to wit, the campaign year and the candidate's party. In more concrete terms, this means that for each campaign year, two files were created, one for each party. The only exception concerns the 1964 and 2000 campaigns. For the latter, no comprehensive collection could be identified, which means that the 2000 campaign is plainly absent from this study. For the former, the Annenberg/Pew Archive collection exploited for this project contains speeches for the Democratic Party only, hence the fact that in total, 27 (and not 28) files have been created.

In order to reduce the number of manipulations and lists of results down to a manageable level, it was decided to compare each of the 27 files against a common reference corpus of general English—instead of against one another—via a procedure known as "key keyword" analysis. The reference corpus used is the open portion from the second release of the American National Corpus (OANC). This portion contains 14,801,441 running words (3,134,962 spoken and 11,666,479 written).

A detailed description of the key keyword analysis falls beyond the scope of this book. The key keyword analysis is yet another sub-category of the keyness analysis procedure described above. The key keyword analysis follows several steps. First, the program *WordList* computes a frequency list for each file of the corpus (27 files in our case). Each of these frequency lists is then compared—via the program *KeyWords*—against the reference corpus frequency list, and 27 keyword lists are generated accordingly. The trick is to use the *batch* function provided by both *WordList* and *KeyWords*. This function drastically reduces the number of operations needed. It only takes *Wordlist* one operation—at least from the researcher's perspective—to compute 27 frequency lists and arrange them within a single batch file. Likewise, it only takes one operation for *KeyWords* to test each file of this batch against the reference norm and create 27 keyword lists, also arranged within one single batch file. A database is then created from this single batch file of keyword lists. It is from this database that the key keyword list is then computed. The key keyword analysis processes the keywords from each of the 27 keyword lists and sorts them out according to their "key keyness value", i.e. the number of files in which a word has been found salient. A word that is a keyword in 27 files has a key keyness value of 27 (or 100%), while a word that is salient in only two files has a key keyness value of 2 (or 7.41%). A word that fails to be statistically salient in at least 2 files does not qualify as a key keyword, although it still qualifies as a keyword, quite logically so since the key keyword analysis is based on a batch of keyword lists. Under the appropriate settings, a key keyword list can contain such file-specific keywords, and therefore makes it possible to extract statistically significant features along a very broad spectrum, ranging from a *being shared by all files* status to a *being totally file specific* status. The key keyword analysis therefore provides a unique opportunity to depart from the case-study approach tradition without rejecting it. The combination of macroscopic and microscopic perspectives that the key keyword analysis gives access to is thus all the more welcome as it seems to offer an answer to a recurrent problem of presidential rhetoric studies, i.e. that "[m]ost of the traditional studies in presidential rhetoric have come in the form of rich case studies. . . . [They] generally fail to provide a coherent body of theory to explain the use of certain rhetorical strategies *within* and *across* presidential administrations [italics mine]" (Warber and Olson 2007: 3).

When computing a key keyword list, one must balance two (sometimes competing) imperatives: (1) choosing a probability value that guarantees that the key keywords obtained are actually valid and significant and (2) choosing a probability value that will not filter out potentially interesting but less salient key keywords and in turn deceivingly lower the actual key keyness value—i.e. the recurrence value—of a key keyword due to too restrictive settings. The probability value (p-value) is the probability that a result is defined as key due to chance only. A probability value of 0.01 means that there is a 1% probability that the item is selected as key due to chance only; p-values range from 0 to 1. The closer to 0, the more certain we are that the difference observed is not the product of mere chance. Setting the p-value closer to 0 will return fewer items, while setting it closer to 1 will add items to the list, but these items will come with a reduced degree of certainty. For the present key keyword analysis of presidential campaign rhetoric, a maximum p-value of 0.001 was chosen, which means that—in the most pessimistic scenario—there is one chance out of a thousand that a keyword is considered significant and salient due to chance only. Such a p-value might sound rather restrictive already, yet it is less so than p-values often used in corpus linguistics.

The key keyword analysis returned no fewer than 9,686 items. A combination of perspectives and methods was in turn used to evaluate how these results could connect to and inform our study of the rhetorical God gap. Among them were concordance reading,[2] collocation analyses[3] and collocation network analyses, keyword analyses, and Bible-specific N-gram identification (see Chapter 4 for further information). In addition to these corpus linguistic techniques, the results were also analyzed and selected on the basis of my knowledge of the American way of religion.[4] While analyzing the results, I tried to consider every rhetorical signal that could be identified as connected to the American-style entanglement of religion and politics. One limitation of the present study is therefore linked to how broad or else limited my knowledge of the USA in general—and of the entanglement of religion and politics in particular—is.

Although it returned a daunting number of items to analyze and categorize, the key keyword analysis has proved highly useful in the quest for the rhetorical God gap as it helped identify party-, time- or even candidate-specific rhetorical features. When needed, the data extracted via the key keyword analysis of the PCS corpus was further enriched by explorations into other specialized corpora, to wit, a corpus of presidential rhetoric (1789–2009, 59.7 million words), Domke and Coe's 1933–2007 corpus of major presidential speeches (Domke and Coe 2008, 1 million words), a corpus of campaign ads (1952–1996, 153,618 words), and a corpus of the National Party Platforms produced by both parties from 1900 to 2008 (764,110 words). The last two corpora were built via the same Annenberg/ Pew Archive database (Kanda Software 2000), while the corpus of presidential rhetoric was extracted from the American Reference Library Database CD-ROM[5] (World Book and Western Standard Publishing Company 2000) and complemented with spoken material from Woolley and Peter's *American Presidency Project* website for the 2001 – 2009 Bush presidency. As for Domke and Coe's corpus, they exploited it in their 2008 book *The God Strategy*. This collection contains 358 "major" presidential speeches (Domke and Coe 2008: 31 and 172), spanning from 1933 to 2007. A detailed list of the speeches selected by Domke and Coe is provided on the companion website to their 2008 book.[6] Assembling these 358 speeches into a corpus was quite easily done via Woolley and Peters's *American Presidency Project* website.

As explained in the introduction, two late additions to these corpora were made while writing Chapters 3 and 4 of the present book. One of the two corpora added to the present study consists of all the primary debates held by both parties during the 2016 presidential campaign (513,646 words, GOP and Democratic Party). Once again, assembling these debates into a corpus was made possible thanks to Woolley and Peters's *American Presidency Project* website. The other corpus—called the Christian Hymn corpus (32,994 words)—contains all of the 242 hymns "published the most frequently in modern hymnals indexed by Hymnary.org" (www.hymnary. org/browse/popular).

## 1.2. Limitations

All research comes with limitations, and the present study is no exception. In what follows, two categories of limitations are briefly discussed. The first category relates to the corpora on which this study relies, while the second category concerns the research methodology. In what comes next, I consider each category in turn.

### 1.2.1. *Limitations Related to the Corpora*

A first limitation of the 1952–2008 PCS corpus lies in the timeframe that it covers, which spans from 1952 to 2008 "only". I certainly do not want to play the pre-modern/modern presidency dichotomy card (see for e.g.

Medhurst (ed.) 1996, 2008; Teten 2005: 6) and claim that there is little use in focusing on public communication from earlier times as it was—so goes the theory—virtually non-existent. Although it seems reasonable to posit the existence of significant differences separating the various ways politicians have gone public through time, the concept of a "modern" rhetorical presidency can mislead one into assuming that only the more recent rhetorical moves deserve being analyzed. Also, and more importantly, the marriage of politics and religion in the U.S. is as old as the nation itself. It follows that our understanding of the rhetorical God gap would most probably be enriched by a study of older sources of political discourse.

In the same line of thought, one might regret the absence of primary election material, with the exception of a cursory analysis of 2016 primary debates in Chapter 3. It does not seem unreasonable to posit that the roles played by religion in primary elections differ from those observed in general campaigns. Indeed, primary elections constitute a different stage where the religious-political interplay unfolds before another kind of audience, with another kind of opponent to defeat, and probably according to a slightly different set of rules. The same kind of regrets can be voiced about the absence of consideration of vice-presidential candidates—who are an important part of the campaign team—or about the choice not to study campaign debates. The truth certainly is that understanding how both parties have exploited religion in their campaign communications implies studying many other sources than mere speeches. These may include newspapers (see Laracey 2004), phone calls, flyers, emails, social media or campaign posters. This similarly applies to the other means of campaign communications, even those that one would describe as non-verbal, visual or symbolic.

In summary, no matter how large the corpora used for this study are, they only give access to one facet of a multi-faceted and quite complex phenomenon. Also, and perhaps more importantly, one should remember that to a very large extent, the specialized corpora used in the present research are only representative of themselves. No matter how much data-based information they can help retrieve and analyze—and this is a lot indeed—and irrespective of how important it is to take such information into account, one should be highly cautious of any kind of hasty extrapolations and sweeping conclusions that go beyond what is actually present in the data.

### *1.2.2. Limitations Related to the Methodology*

The bottom-up corpus-driven approach taken here leaves little place for potentially enlightening questions if they are not introduced by the data itself. However, there is little doubt that top-down analyses deserve to be run as well, notably (but not exclusively) around items that are not necessarily quantitatively salient, but potentially enlightening nonetheless. In the same line of thought, our approach is not primarily concerned with—nor actually devised to study—cases where playing the religious card would mean refraining from using religious language. A study of significantly less frequent items is actually possible with a keyness analysis procedure and should perhaps be part of future research efforts in order to better understand the kind of language that candidates—taken altogether as well as individually—have preferred to avoid. Tracking down silence and what is not said is probably a trickier but no less important enterprise because—as Baker and Partington both point out—silence can also be quite revealing (Baker 2006: 19; Partington 2013: 294–295).

Another limitation of this study results from its scope and the fact that it qualifies as a first step in the study of the rhetorical God gap. Given the very large amount of data returned by our approach and the variety of patterns that it helped unearth, and because of the impossibility of treating all the aspects pertaining to the rhetorical God gap within one book, choices had to be made regarding what to further explore and report. This in turn means that we may have missed out on some important aspects of the rhetorical God gap and barely scratched the surface of others. This also means that there is undoubtedly room for future research to complement our own.

The statistical measurements and quantitative comparisons that are reported here mostly rely on normalized frequencies per N words. Even though this is actually standard practice in corpus linguistics, relying on normalized frequencies exclusively may keep some trends undetected and in turn potentially skew the interpretation of data. Another normalization basis might offer another lens through which other types of comparison can be made and differences identified. Relying on a "per speech" count rather than on a per N words count is an approach that Domke and Coe followed in their book *The God Strategy* (2008), and I believe this might constitute an approach that is complementary to our own.

## Notes

1. www.presidentialrhetoric.com/campaign/index.html (Last consulted: March 18, 2018).
2. A concordance analysis is "simply a list of all of the occurrences of a particular search term in a corpus, presented within the context that they occur in; usually a few words to the left and right of the search term" (Baker 2006: 71).
3. Collocation: "A co-occurrence relationship between words or phrases. Words are said to *collocate* with one another if one is more likely to occur in the presence of the other than elsewhere" (CASS Briefings 2013: 4).
4. For the sake of transparency—and although a university degree does not guarantee good knowledge or intelligence—I want to inform the reader that I hold an advanced master in American Studies from the University of Antwerp (Belgium) and that I devoted my MA thesis to the religious rhetoric of U.S. presidents. It is only after I completed that MA thesis and considered the possibility of a PhD

research project that I discovered corpus linguistics and what it could bring to the field.
5. The American Reference Library Database contains three collections of presidential rhetoric, i.e. (1) *The Messages and Papers of the Presidents* spreading from George Washington (1789–1797) to William Howard Taft (1909–1913); (2) *The Public Papers of the Presidents of the United States*, spanning from President Herbert Hoover (1929–1933) up to the 1993 Clinton presidency; and (3) *The Weekly Compilation of Presidential Documents*, all containing Clinton's rhetoric up to 1999. Several presidents are missing: Woodrow Wilson (1913–1921), Warren G. Harding (1921–1923) and Calvin Coolidge (1923–1929).
6. i.e. www.thegodstrategy.com. For the list of speeches, see www.thegodstrategy.com/documents/AppendixA.pdf (Broken link. Last consulted: May 25, 2014).

# References

*The American Presidency Project*. Website. University of California, Santa Barbara. www.presidency.ucsb.edu/ Last consulted: July 12, 2018.

Baker, P. 2006. *Using Corpora in Discourse Analysis*. London: Continuum.

CASS Briefings. 2013. Corpus linguistics: some key terms. Lancaster: The ESRC Centre for Corpus Approaches to Social Science, Lancaster University, UK. Retrieved from http://cass.lancs.ac.uk/cass-briefings/ Last consulted: July 18, 2019.

Domke, D. and Coe, K. 2008. *The God Strategy: How Religion Became a Political Weapon in America*. New York: Oxford University Press.

Guerini, M., Strapparava, C. and Stock, O. 2008. CORPS: A Corpus of Tagged Political Speeches for Persuasive Communication Processing. *Journal of Information Technology & Politics*, Vol. 5, No. 1, 19–32, Routledge.

Hymnary.*org*. Website. https://hymnary.org/ Last consulted: October 15, 2018.

Kanda Software, Inc. 2000. *The Annenberg/Pew Archive of Presidential Campaign Discourse*. (Version 1.0) [Computer software]. The Annenberg School for Communication, University of Pennsylvania.

Laracey, M. 2004. *Who Listened? Political Media Communications by "Pre-Modern" Presidents*. Paper prepared for presentation at the Annual Meeting of the Midwest Political Science Association, Chicago, April 15–18.

Medhurst, M. J. (ed.). 1996. *Beyond the Rhetorical Presidency*. College Station, TX: Texas A&M University Press.

Medhurst, M. J. (ed.). 2008. *Before the Rhetorical Presidency*. College Station, TX: Texas A&M University Press.

Partington, A. 2013. Evaluating Evaluation and Some Concluding Thoughts on CADS. In Morley, J. and Bayley, P. (eds.). *Corpus-Assisted Discourse Studies on the Iraq Conflict: Wording the War*. Abingdon, Oxon: Routledge, 261–303.

*PresidentialRhetoric.com*. Website. www.presidentialrhetoric.com/index.html Last consulted: July 12, 2018.

Scott, M. 2008. *Word Smith Tools* (Version 5). Liverpool: Lexical Analysis Software.

Teten, R. L. 2005. *The Modern Rhetorical Presidency Reconsidered: Policy Proposal and Advocacy in Presidential State of the Union Addresses from George Washington to George W. Bush*. Paper prepared for delivery at the 2005 annual meeting of the American Political Science Association, Washington, DC, September 1–4.

Vincent, A. 2014. *A Corpus Linguistics Approach to the Rhetorical God Gap in U.S. Presidential Campaigns*. Unpublished PhD thesis. Louvain-la-Neuve: Centre for English Corpus Linguistics, Université Catholique de Louvain.

Warber, A. L. and Olson, L. R. 2007. *Religion and Ronald Reagan's Rhetorical Presidency*. Paper presented at the annual meeting of the American Political Science Association, Hyatt Regency Chicago and the Sheraton Chicago Hotel and Towers, Chicago, IL, August 30.

World Book and Western Standard Publishing Company. 2000. *American Reference Library* (Version 4.20). [CD-Rom]. Orem, UT: Western Standard Publishing Company.

# 2 Religious Rhetoric in the Early Cold War

The 1956 movie *The Ten Commandments* is probably best remembered for its cast of celebrities, its impressive visual effects, and for it becoming a religiously tinted seasonal tradition in many families. One thing it might be much less remembered for, however, is its quite unusual prologue delivered by Director Cecil B. DeMille himself. DeMille appeared from behind curtains on stage and claimed:

> The theme of this picture is whether men ought to be ruled by God's law or whether they are to be ruled by the whims of a dictator like Rameses. Are men the property of the state, or are they free souls under God? The same battle continues throughout the world today.

Through this prologue, DeMille offered the audience a clear indication that the Cold War, pitting America—free and under God—against godless Communism, was nothing less than a re-enactment of biblical Exodus (Gunn 2009: 69–72; Reinhartz 2013: 37; Romanowski 2017: 429; Shaw 2003: 217). DeMille was certainly not alone in his tapping into biblical metaphors to fuel the anti-communist propaganda. Consider for example how Democratic Party candidate John Kennedy emulated DeMille's Manichean depiction of the world and how he presented the 1960 election as boiling down to a very similar polarity between freedom and slavery:

> I think the great question in the election of 1960. . . is whether the world will exist half slave or half free, or whether we will begin to move in the direction of freedom or in the direction of slavery. . . . Therefore, the issues in this campaign, in a very real sense, transcend the traditional issues which have separated our two parties. The great question now for all Americans, regardless of party, is whether they can make freedom work, whether they can make this system work in a difficult and dangerous period, whether they can demonstrate to a watching world

that we represent the way to the future and the Communist system represents a system as old as Egypt.

(Kennedy, September 9, 1960. Shrine Auditorium Speech, Los Angeles)

If anything, both DeMille's very personal introduction to *The Ten Commandments* and Kennedy's words quoted above offer a very enlightening backdrop against which to understand the way early Cold War presidential candidates—on both sides of the political spectrum—would articulate the Cold War through pretty much the same religiously tinted language and biblical metaphors. This contextual background will therefore be quite helpful in the interpretation of the Cold-War-related results extracted via our key keyword analysis. The importance of this Cold-War-related context notwithstanding, one must understand that the biblically inspired storyline deployed against godless Communism did not appear out of the blue nor was it germane to the Cold War era only. Instead, it was reminiscent of a rationale set in place from the very birth of the Nation, and which presented the settlers as God's chosen people on a mission to build the new Promised Land. The Exodus theme was again tapped into to justify the 19th-century Westward Expansion and cloak it under the pretence of America's Manifest Destiny.

The present research has helped identify several patterns that are direct products of the early Cold War context, which was marked by an intense exploitation of religion as a weapon against Communism (see for e.g. Gunn 2009; Inboden 2008; Kirby (ed) 2003). More specifically, the key keyword, concordance and collocation analyses runs have helped dig out an early-Cold-War-specific insistence—in campaign rhetoric—on slavery (Table 2.1), atheism (Table 2.2) and on the terms *crusade* (Table 2.3), *soul, souls, spiritual* and *spiritually* (Table 2.4).[1]

*Table 2.1* Slavery Pattern (Key keyword analysis, PCS corpus, rel. freq. per 1,000 words)

| Republican Party | Year | Democratic Party |
|---|---|---|
| slave (0.04), enslaved (0.03), enslavement (0.01) | 1952 | bondage (0.02), enslave (0.009), enslaved (0.03) |
| enslaved (0.04) | 1956 | – |
| slavery (0.04), enslave (0.007), enslaved (0.03) | 1960 | slave (0.12), slavery (0.07) |
| no 1964 GOP file | 1964 | slavery (0.09) |
| – | from 1968 to 1980 | – |
| – | 1984 | bondage (0.03) |
| – | from 1988 to 2008 | – |

*Table 2.2* Atheism Pattern (Key keyword analysis, PCS corpus, rel. freq. per 1,000 words)

| Republican Party | Year | Democratic Party |
|---|---|---|
| godless (0.03), atheistic (0.02) | 1952 | – |
| – | 1956 | – |
| atheistic (0.04) | 1960 | – |
| no 1964 GOP file | from 1964 to 2008 | – |

*Table 2.3* Crusade Pattern (Key keyword analysis, PCS corpus, rel. freq. per 1,000 words)

| Republican Party | Year | Democratic Party |
|---|---|---|
| crusade (1.21) | 1952 | crusade (0.17) |
| – | 1956 | crusade (0.06) |
| crusade (0.06) | 1960 | – |
| no 1964 GOP file | from 1964 to 1988 | – |
| crusade (0.03) | 1992 | – |
| – | from 1996 to 2008 | – |

*Table 2.4* Soul/Spirituality Pattern (Key keyword analysis, PCS corpus, rel. freq. per 1,000 words)

| Republican Party | Year | Democratic Party |
|---|---|---|
| souls (0.06), spiritual (0.32), spiritually (0.06) | 1952 | soul (0.07), souls (0.04) |
| spiritual (0.25) | 1956 | spiritual (0.08) |
| souls (0.05), spiritual (0.22), spiritually (0.03) | 1960 | – |
| no 1964 GOP file | 1964 | – |
| – | 1968 | – |
| spiritual (0.10) | 1972 | soul (0.09), souls (0.04) |
| – | from 1976 to 1996 | – |
| soul (0.29), souls (0.09) | 2004 | – |
| – | 2008 | – |

In spite of the important role played by religion in the struggle against Communism, one can deplore the fact that "[t]o date . . . religion's place in Cold War historiography has been systematically neglected" (Kirby 2003: 1). The patterns returned here provide quantitative evidence that—in campaign rhetoric at least—the salience of a certain ideological language against Communism is real.

In what follows, two excerpts are provided in order to put our cold-war-related findings back into their rhetorical context and illustrate how these salient words would be articulated in such a way as to acquire an unmistakably ideological—and very often religious—tone:

> While the anti-Christ stalks around, organized Communism seeks even to dethrone God from His central place in this universe. It attempts to uproot everywhere it goes the gentle and restraining influences of the religion of love and peace. One by one the lamps of civilization go out and nameless horrors are perpetrated in darkness. All this is done by an enemy of a kind that we have never faced before. He is primitive but he is also advanced. He goes with a piece of black bread in his hand, but in his mind he carries the awful knowledge of atomic energy. He is careful, cool, calculating, and he counts time not impatiently like we do, not by the clock, but by decades, in terms of centuries. . . . The task that confronts us will try our souls. It will exact a high price in discipline of mind and in austerity of spirit. . . . Long ago we asserted a great principle on this continent: that men are, and of right ought to be, free. Now we are called upon to defend that right against the mightiest forces of evil ever assembled under the sun. This is a time to think, a time to feel, a time to pray. We shall need all of the resources of the stubborn mind, the stout heart, the soul refreshed, in the task that confronts us. . . . You and you alone will decide the fate of your family and your country for decades to come. You will decide whether you are to be slaves or free—to live gloriously, or perish miserably. . . . Your salvation is in your hands; in the stubbornness of your minds, the tenacity of your hearts, and such blessings as God, sorely tried by His children, shall give us.
>
> (Stevenson, September 29, 1952. Station
> WGN-NBC-TV speech)

As implied earlier, such rhetoric is not representative of Democratic Party candidate Stevenson alone, but crosses party lines, as illustrated by the words uttered by Eisenhower a few weeks later:

> World War II was a crusade to defeat the evil, sinister threat of dicta-torial domination. . . . But as the years have passed since the end of that crusade, the lights of our world have been going out again, year after year. What happened? . . . This terrible danger is Godless Com-munism. . . . But great as this threat is, and vigilant as we must eternally be to stand together with our friends of the free world, we also know in our hearts that there is no force in this world so vital or so strong, when

> given corresponding leadership, as the American people. . . . [W]e have a spiritual strength beyond the enemy's reach or understanding. It is the strength of people who believe that man is made in the image of God. But, if we are to win this deadly struggle with Communism, we must have a leadership that can unite us behind great objectives—a leadership morally and spiritually strong. The best that is within us Americans will respond to a calling of high purpose. . . . This struggle between Communism and freedom is a struggle of ideas. To win in such a battle, our ideas must be better. And our idea must come alive through the positive, moral vitality of our leadership. . . . The evil of Communism must be fought on many fronts. . . . We can conquer Communism, if we have a leadership of high purpose and moral stamina, a leadership that draws strength from its spiritual faith. And it is to seek out these qualities and place them at the nation's helm that my associate and I have embarked upon this second crusade, this "Crusade in America." . . . A strong America, a well-governed America, an America that is morally and spiritually sound, is the best answer to the evil threat of cynicism and lack of self-respect within, and to the evil threat of Communism without. If you believe that as I do, will you join our crusade?
>
> (Eisenhower, October 21, 1952. Speech in Boston, Massachusetts)

The "atheism gap" (Table 2.2) between the GOP and a statistically silent Democratic Party is an unexpected observation. The multi-word query *atheis*/godless/nonbeliev*/non believ** in the 1952–2008 Presidential Campaign Speeches corpus[2] (using WordSmith's *Concord* tool) shows that the Democrats have not gone totally silent about atheism, although in the Democratic Party camp, the *atheis** node has been used much later, and appears in the Obama file only (see Figure 2.1).

Interrogating our corpus of presidential rhetoric (1789–2009) with *Concord* (same multi-word query) reveals a similar time-cum-party gap. Except for one *atheis** hit in the President Ulysses Grant file (1869–1877)

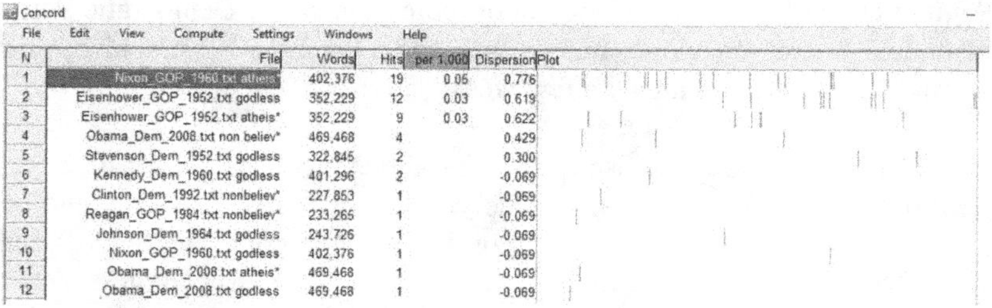
Concord
File Edit View Compute Settings Windows Help

| N | File | Words | Hits | per 1,000 | Dispersion | Plot |
|---|---|---|---|---|---|---|
| 1 | Nixon_GOP_1960.txt atheis* | 402,376 | 19 | 0.05 | 0.776 | |
| 2 | Eisenhower_GOP_1952.txt godless | 352,229 | 12 | 0.03 | 0.619 | |
| 3 | Eisenhower_GOP_1952.txt atheis* | 352,229 | 9 | 0.03 | 0.622 | |
| 4 | Obama_Dem_2008.txt non believ* | 469,468 | 4 | | 0.429 | |
| 5 | Stevenson_Dem_1952.txt godless | 322,845 | 2 | | 0.300 | |
| 6 | Kennedy_Dem_1960.txt godless | 401,296 | 2 | | -0.069 | |
| 7 | Clinton_Dem_1992.txt nonbeliev* | 227,853 | 1 | | -0.069 | |
| 8 | Reagan_GOP_1984.txt nonbeliev* | 233,265 | 1 | | -0.069 | |
| 9 | Johnson_Dem_1964.txt godless | 243,726 | 1 | | -0.069 | |
| 10 | Nixon_GOP_1960.txt godless | 402,376 | 1 | | -0.069 | |
| 11 | Obama_Dem_2008.txt atheis* | 469,468 | 1 | | -0.069 | |
| 12 | Obama_Dem_2008.txt godless | 469,468 | 1 | | -0.069 | |

*Figure 2.1* Statistics returned from the query *atheis*/godless/nonbeliev*/non believ** in the 1952–2008 PCS corpus

and another similar hit in the Franklin D. Roosevelt file (1933–1945), all other occurrences returned by the multi-word query (i.e. 116 out of 118 hits) are located in the post WWII era. References to *nonbeliever\** (7 hits, no hit returned for *non believ\**) are introduced from the Nixon 1969–1974 presidency on,[3] and most hits returned for the two other queried nodes (*atheis\** and *godless*, 109 hits in total) are produced by the first two Cold War Presidents, i.e. Truman (a Democrat, 19 hits, rel. freq. 0.005 per 1,000 words) and Eisenhower (a Republican, 42 hits, rel. freq. 0.015 per 1,000 words). These two presidents show the highest relative frequency and dispersion value scores for the combined query *atheis\*/ godless*, which means that not only did they use these references the most, but they also used them more recurrently than all the other presidents. The relative frequency gap between Eisenhower and Truman is significant ($X^2 = 12.77181$, difference is significant at $p < 0.001$). These time and party differences in presidential rhetoric parallel the patterns observed in presidential campaign rhetoric (Table 2.2). Using the same multi-word query in the 1900–2008 National Party Platforms corpus (5 hits) confirms that the language around atheism is, to a very large extent, an early Cold War phenomenon directed against Communism and mostly produced by the Republican Party (Figure 2.2).[4]

Given the geopolitical context, much of the surprise elicited by Table 2.2 actually resides in the absence of salient references to atheism on the part of the early Cold War Democratic Party candidates. Neither Table 2.2 nor the multi-word query conducted in the PCS corpus (Figure 2.1), the Presidential Rhetoric corpus or the National Party Platforms corpus (Figure 2.2) suggest an enduring gap between both parties. In other words, if talk of an atheism gap in campaign speeches is allowed and backed up by evidence, it must be described as a gap that is located in a very specific period and that tilts the balance in favour of two GOP candidates (Eisenhower 1952 and Nixon 1960) rather than in favour of the entire Republican Party.

Table 2.3 may appear quite counterintuitive, at least for those who—in the post 9/11 context—had been alarmed by George W. Bush's use of the crusade reference, which they often believed to be unique, and which was cast by some media outlets—sometimes in the form of quite evocative

| N | Concordance | Set | File |
|---|---|---|---|
| 1 | of a regime dominated by international, atheistic Communism in the Western Hemisphere | atheis* | Democratic Platform of 1960 TXT |
| 2 | and defeat their objective of establishing here a godless dictatorship controlled from abroad. We | godless | Republican Platform of 1948 TXT |
| 3 | countless human beings to a despotism and godless terrorism, which in turn enables the | godless | Republican Platform of 1952 TXT |
| 4 | within the Soviet Bloc challenge the brutal and atheistic doctrines of Soviet Communism. For | atheis* | Republican Platform of 1956 TXT |
| 5 | The supreme challenge to this policy is an atheistic imperialism-Communism. Our nation's | atheis* | Republican Platform of 1964 TXT |

*Figure 2.2* Concordance lines (5 hits) returned from the query *atheis\*/godless/non-believ\*/non believ\** in the 1900–2008 National Party Platforms corpus, 1900–2008, both parties

photomontages[5]—as supporting evidence that Bush was a modern day crusader driven by a religious-cum-hegemonic agenda.

Even Boston University Professor Stephen Prothero—who authored a highly recommendable and instructive book on the religious illiteracy of his fellow Americans—seemingly falls prey to the same reductive shortcut in the definition of "crusades" that he provides in his appended Dictionary of Religious Literacy. Prothero first describes the medieval roots of the crusades. Strikingly enough, he then concludes his historical definition by mentioning President George W. Bush's reference "to the war on terrorism as a 'crusade'" (2007: 214), while keeping totally silent about the fact that, however politically debatable, Bush's crusade reference was far from unprecedented in American political language. Such silence sounds like an implicit confession that Prothero actually concurs with the traditional—but misinformed—depiction of Bush as the unprecedented crusader.

Table 2.3 reminds us that *crusade* is not unique to George W. Bush and also shows that the Bush 2004 campaign speeches file is actually not even marked by a significant usage of this word. As will become apparent in the next figure (Figure 2.4), no hit for the query *crusad** was actually found in Bush's 2004 campaign speeches.[6] Also, Table 2.3 brings important quantitative evidence against Domke and Coe's claim that the term *crusade* occurs four times more frequently from 1981 on. In turn, our findings challenge Domke and Coe's depiction of the term *crusade* as the sole product of a religiously charged electoral strategy specifically located in the 1981 onwards era (Domke and Coe 2008: 41–42). This erroneous conclusion is mostly due to the size and representativeness of the corpus analyzed by Domke and Coe (see how Figure 2.3 compares to Figures 2.4 and 2.5 in terms of raw and relative frequencies, with the case of Eisenhower being quite telling) or else due to conclusions about electoral strategies that go far beyond what is actually observed. Combining Table 2.3 with the more precise quantitative measures returned from the query *crusad** in our corpus of campaign speeches (1952–2008, Figure 2.4), our corpus of presidential rhetoric (1789–2009, Figure 2.5) and our National Party Platforms corpus (1900–2008, Figure 2.6) brings a more complete—and more complex—picture.

| N | File | Words | Hits | per 1,000 | Dispersion Plot |
|---|------|-------|------|-----------|-----------------|
| 1 | Reagan Ronald 1981 to 1989.TXT | 149,861 | | 0.327 | |
| 2 | Bush G H W 1989 to 1993.TXT | 56,525 | | 0.260 | |
| 3 | Clinton William J 1993 to 2001.txt | 103,777 | | 0.478 | |
| 4 | Roosevelt Franklin Delano 1933 to 1945.TXT | 141,975 | | 0.300 | |
| 5 | Nixon Richard 1969 to 1974.TXT | 112,220 | | -0.069 | |
| 6 | Eisenhower Dwight 1953 to 1961.TXT | 139,664 | | -0.069 | |

*Figure 2.3* Statistics returned by the query *crusad** in Domke and Coe's Corpus of Major Presidential Speeches (1933–2007)

**Concord**

File  Edit  View  Compute  Settings  Windows  Help

| N | File | Words | Hits | per 1,000 | Dispersion | Plot |
|---|------|-------|------|-----------|------------|------|
| 1 | Eisenhower_GOP_1952.txt | 352,229 | 432 | 1.2 | 0.721 | |
| 2 | Stevenson_Dem_1952.txt | 322,845 | 60 | 0.19 | 0.742 | |
| 3 | Stevenson_Dem_1956.txt | 144,313 | 13 | 0.09 | 0.570 | |
| 4 | Nixon_GOP_1960.txt | 402,376 | 26 | 0.06 | 0.536 | |
| 5 | Eisenhower_GOP_1956.txt | 68,560 | 4 | 0.06 | 0.300 | |
| 6 | Mondale_Dem_1984.txt | 115,177 | 4 | 0.03 | -0.069 | |
| 7 | Reagan_GOP_1980.txt | 87,732 | 3 | 0.03 | 0.250 | |
| 8 | Bush_GOP_1992.txt | 269,425 | 8 | 0.03 | 0.544 | |
| 9 | Ford_GOP_1976.txt | 144,270 | 4 | 0.03 | 0.429 | |
| 10 | Nixon_GOP_1972.txt | 110,124 | 3 | 0.03 | 0.250 | |
| 11 | Carter_1976.txt | 110,682 | 3 | 0.03 | 0.250 | |
| 12 | Clinton_Dem_1992.txt | 227,853 | 6 | 0.03 | 0.644 | |
| 13 | Carter_Dem_1980.txt | 193,105 | 4 | 0.02 | 0.429 | |
| 14 | Kennedy_Dem_1960.txt | 401,296 | 6 | 0.01 | 0.300 | |
| 15 | Reagan_GOP_1984.txt | 233,265 | 3 | 0.01 | 0.250 | |
| 16 | Johnson_Dem_1964.txt | 243,726 | 3 | 0.01 | 0.250 | |
| 17 | Bush_GOP_1988.txt | 83,105 | 1 | 0.01 | -0.069 | |
| 18 | Clinton_Dem_1996.txt | 338,930 | | | 0.250 | |
| 19 | McGovern_Dem_1972.txt | 159,515 | | | -0.069 | |
| 20 | Nixon_GOP_1968.txt | 201,504 | | | -0.069 | |
| 21 | McCain_GOP_2008.txt | 276,619 | | | -0.069 | |
| 22 | Humphrey_Dem_1968.txt | 429,150 | | | -0.069 | |

*Figure 2.4* Statistics returned by the query *crusad\** in the Presidential Campaign Speeches corpus (1952–2008)

**Concord**

File  Edit  View  Compute  Settings  Windows  Help

| N | File | Words | Hits | per 1,000 | Dispersion | Plot |
|---|------|-------|------|-----------|------------|------|
| 1 | 33 Truman Harry 1945 1953 TXT | 3,226,053 | 144 | 0.04 | 0.580 | |
| 2 | 41 Bush George HW 1989 1993 TXT | 4,646,409 | 149 | 0.03 | 0.742 | |
| 3 | 34 Eisenhower Dwight 1953 1961 TXT | 2,667,073 | 67 | 0.03 | 0.726 | |
| 4 | 40 Reagan Ronald 1981 1989 TXT | 7,736,177 | 165 | 0.02 | 0.676 | |
| 5 | 13 Fillmore Millard 1850 1853 TXT | 59,238 | 1 | 0.02 | -0.069 | |
| 6 | 36 Johnson Lyndon B 1963 1969 TXT | 3,843,098 | 52 | 0.01 | 0.811 | |
| 7 | 42 Clinton William 1993 up to 1999 TXT | 11,801,170 | 113 | | 0.785 | |
| 8 | 15 Buchanan James 1857 1861 TXT | 117,468 | 1 | | -0.069 | |
| 9 | 32 Roosevelt Franklin D 1933 1945 TXT | 1,905,159 | 15 | | 0.669 | |
| 10 | 16 Lincoln Abraham 1861 1865 TXT | 127,504 | 1 | | -0.069 | |
| 11 | 37 Nixon Richard 1969 1974 TXT | 3,360,732 | 25 | | 0.864 | |
| 12 | 38 Ford Gerald 1974 1977 TXT | 2,441,409 | 15 | | 0.706 | |
| 13 | 39 Carter James 1977 1981 TXT | 5,242,875 | 28 | | 0.695 | |
| 14 | 22 Cleveland Grover 1885 1889 TXT | 253,244 | 1 | | -0.069 | |
| 15 | 31 Hoover Herbert 1929 1933 TXT | 869,871 | 1 | | -0.069 | |
| 16 | 35 Kennedy John 1961 1963 TXT | 1,600,516 | 4 | | 0.192 | |
| 17 | 26 Roosevelt Theodore 1901 1909 TXT | 500,408 | 1 | | -0.069 | |
| 18 | 43 Bush GW 2001 2009 txt | 5,571,792 | 10 | | 0.580 | |

*Figure 2.5* Statistics returned by the query *crusad\** in the Presidential Rhetoric corpus (1789–2009)

**Concord**

File  Edit  View  Compute  Settings  Windows  Help

| N | File | Words | Hits | per 1,000 | Dispersion | Plot |
|---|------|-------|------|-----------|------------|------|
| 1 | Republican Platform of 1992 TXT | 28,538 | 6 | 0.21 | 0.300 | |
| 2 | Republican Platform of 1964 TXT | 8,726 | 1 | 0.11 | -0.069 | |
| 3 | Republican Platform of 1968 TXT | 9,973 | 1 | 0.10 | -0.069 | |
| 4 | Republican Platform of 1996 TXT | 30,381 | 3 | 0.10 | 0.478 | |
| 5 | Republican Platform of 1960 TXT | 10,663 | 1 | 0.09 | -0.069 | |
| 6 | Republican Platform of 1988 TXT | 36,308 | 1 | 0.08 | -0.069 | |
| 7 | Democratic Platform of 2000.txt | 24,228 | 2 | 0.08 | 0.300 | |
| 8 | Democratic Platform of 1956 TXT | 12,851 | 1 | 0.08 | -0.069 | |
| 9 | Republican Platform of 1984 TXT | 27,996 | 1 | 0.04 | -0.069 | |
| 10 | Republican Platform of 1980 TXT | 34,552 | 1 | 0.03 | -0.069 | |

*Figure 2.6* Statistics returned by the query *crusad\** in the National Party Platforms Corpus (1900–2008)

Two main trends transpire from Figures 2.4, 2.5 and 2.6 (the results are sorted by relative frequency order). On the one hand, Figures 2.5 and 2.6—which spread in aggregate over more than 200 years—show that the crusade reference is mostly located in the post WWII era. Figure 2.4—and to a lesser extent Figure 2.5—show that the Cold War era ranks in a prominent position on this post-WWII time span. Figures 2.5 and 2.6 indicate that the crusade reference gained new prominence around the 1980s and 1990s, but Figures 2.4 and 2.5 clearly indicate that failing to recognize the importance of the Cold War era is a misleading omission. Another trend that is apparent in Figure 2.6 is that of a party gap of sorts where the GOP appears more inclined to integrate the word *crusade* into its political manifesto, and this in a recurrent fashion from 1960 onwards. The chances are that this official usage indicates a certain level of affection for the crusade reference on the part of GOP members, which in turn might shed some light upon the reasons why George W. Bush—who ranks lowest in Figure 2.5 and is totally absent from Figure 2.4—used the crusade term to articulate his views in the aftermath of the 9/11 attacks. This potential affection for the crusade reference might also result from or connect to the particularly high frequency observed for Eisenhower in Table 2.3 and Figure 2.4. Such a high frequency in Eisenhower's 1952 campaign rhetoric sets him clearly apart from the rest, and the difference with the second highest score in Figure 2.4 (i.e. Stevenson 1952) is highly significant ($X^2 = 249.04724$, difference is significant at $p < 0.001$). The difference with the other candidates is logically even greater. In the future, more research attention should be devoted to Eisenhower's campaign rhetoric and this crusade gap in order to understand the reasons underlying Eisenhower's frequent usage of the term *crusade* and the consequences it might have had on the later rhetoric produced by the GOP. For the sake of contextual precision, it must be added that Eisenhower's affection for the term *crusade* apparently predates his 1952 campaign bid, as attested by the very title of his 1948 book *Crusade in Europe*. Also, it must be noted that other figures who gained prominence during the early Cold War context did exploit the crusade reference as well, like Billy Graham, who is now considered as an unmistakable figure of the American-style political religious entanglement (see for example Fath 2004: 65–66 and 89–92).

Reading the concordance lines returned from the different corpora reveals that the term *crusade* has been used on many occasions by American politicians, and quite often—although not always—with a far less religious undertone than some commentators on the European side of the Atlantic are willing to believe. Skimming through the concordance lines from the query *crusade* in the 1952–2008 PCS corpus returns examples like *crusade against crime* (Carter 1976), *crusade against drugs* (Clinton 1996), *crusade for change* (Clinton 1992), *crusade for human rights* (Kennedy

1960), *crusade for the kind of government that our forefathers gave us* (Ford 1976), *anti-cancer crusade* (Nixon 1972), *crusade to get rid of that administration* (Reagan 1980), *crusade to keep this nation on the road to peace* (Carter 1980), *crusade to lift the standard of life for all Americans* (McGovern 1972), *crusade to make America great again*[7] (Reagan 1980 and 1984), *crusade to raise standards, to free the teachers* (Bush 1992), *crusade to rebuild America* (Clinton 1992), *crusade to renew America* (Bush 1992), *crusade to restore in our schools needed discipline* (Reagan 1984), or—to put an end to this non-exhaustive list—*crusade to save our children [from drugs]* (Nixon 1972). It seems that *crusade* appears as much of a multi-usage rhetorical tool as the equally militarily-sounding term *war*, which has been used within the same kind of slogan-like phrases boasting about waging war on/against *terror, drugs, poverty, crime, terrorism, hunger, waste, Islamic terrorists, drug, narcotics, violent extremists, California, AIDS, heroin, organized crime* or *inflation*.[8] For those willing to find examples where the crusade imagery took on true religious meanings while serving geopolitical concerns, Kirby (2003: 5) and Inboden (2008: location 115–121 of 5301) define the Cold War as the right period to consider.

Parenthetically but interestingly, another pattern identified in this research—but not detailed in the present book—emulates the distribution of *crusade* as it mostly comes in two similar waves, the first of which is in direct link with the Cold War context. This pattern relates to the term *judeo* and the definition of America as a Judeo-Christian nation. Although the debate about supposed Christian roots of the American Nation has been raging since its very birth (see for example Church 2002, 2007; Espinosa (ed.) 2009: 3–5; Hunter 1991; Meacham 2007) and is therefore not limited to a single era, our study of the PCS corpus and of our other specialized corpora revealed a cold-war-related usage of the phrase *judeo-christian* to serve as an ecumenical and consensual call from both parties to fight against godless communism. Around the 1970s, the story of a Judeo-Christian America became far more partisan and served a new type of fight—now domestic rather than foreign—against a new type of enemy, i.e. "the liberals". This modification in tone was the product of the Republicans' defence of their conservative agenda—which they defined as inspired by the Judeo-Christian tradition—against the liberal agenda. (for more on the Judeo-Christian pattern, see Vincent 2014: 163–198).

Much like Table 2.3, Table 2.5 next offers a counterintuitive reminder that George W. Bush did not have an absolute monopoly on the term *evil*, which is however believed to be specific to Bush's codeword strategy to "[connect] deeply with co-religionists while flying under the radar of non-religious Americans" (Rozell and Das Gupta 2006: 19).[9] Among others, Table 2.5 shows that the early Cold War is marked by a salient reference to *evil* that crosses party lines.[10] Reading the concordance lines for this era

*Table 2.5* Evil Pattern (Key keyword analysis, PCS corpus, rel. freq. per 1,000 words)

| Republican Party | Year | Democratic Party |
| --- | --- | --- |
| evil (0.09) | 1952 | evil (0.13) |
| – | 1956 | – |
| – | 1960 | – |
| no 1964 GOP file | 1964 | evils (0.03) |
| – | from 1968 to 2004 | – |
| evil (0.09) | 2008 | – |

shows that Communism was often at the receiving end of such a Manichean and ideological labelling.

When merged into one comprehensive whole, Tables 2.1 to 2.5 constitute a powerful reminder of the important role that religion played in the ideological warfare against Communism. The religious rhetoric employed back then took rather strong stances, and some of them might sound politically incorrect today. The Cold War religious rhetoric drew on several biblical imageries and depicted a Manichean vision of a world torn apart between America—under God, free, shining, the last best hope of human kind—and an evil communist empire—a reincarnation of Biblical Egypt, a tyrannical and materialistic state where enslaved people would live in darkness and fear. There is no doubt that understanding the entanglement of religion and politics in America cannot be achieved without serious consideration of the ways religion was used during the Cold War. Likewise, those doing research on more recent political and religious discourse in the U.S. would be well advised to consider the deeply religious tone of the Cold War rhetoric before falling prey to the sirens of sensationalism and calling what they observe unprecedented or extraordinary. Finally, and on a more personal note, I believe that future research would make an important contribution if it focused more specifically on a comparison between the rhetoric produced during the ideological warfare of the early Cold War era and the rhetoric produced in the context of the post 9/11 war on Islamic terrorism.[11]

## Coming Next

Since the very birth of the American nation, religion in politics has followed a pendulum swing, alternating between being a force of cohesion and being a partisan and divisive tool. The constant oscillation between these two extremes and the various roles played by religion have always been driven by context. During the early Cold War, religion was primarily used by both parties against the common Communist threat rather than against each other. But as the pendulum metaphor suggests, a modification in trend is always to be expected. Chapter 3 will demonstrate how religion would progressively be exploited as a partisan weapon to fight the so-called culture wars and drive a wedge between the conservatives and their liberal opponents.

## Notes

1. As regards Table 2.4, going through a concordance analysis of its results indicates that the salient occurrences of *soul/souls/spiritual* as of 1972 participated in another kind of rhetoric, most probably linked to what will be described later as the liberal/conservative pattern (see Chapter 3). Likewise, George W. Bush exploited the keyword *soul* in order to claim that the heart and soul of America is not to be found in Hollywood—i.e. the liberal side—but to be found "in caring communities like Toledo, Ohio" (Bush, October 29, 2004) or any other communities he found fit to appeal to.
2. The wildcard function—represented by the * symbol—makes *Concord* search for every possible inflected form of the queried root.
3. *nonbeliever** is to be found in Nixon 1969–1974 (2 hits), Reagan 1981–1989 (4 hits) and Clinton 1993–1999 (1 hit).
4. History tells us that playing the atheism card in politics is however not limited solely to the early Cold War era. Probably the most famous example is to be found back in the 1800 presidential campaign opposing Jefferson against Adams. Both camps engaged in negative campaigning that might actually make current negative campaigns appear quite decent and polite in comparison. The Adams camp notably attacked Jefferson for being a dangerous atheist (see for example Church 2007: 187–193; Lambert 1997: 769–792; Swint 2008: 183–191). However, an additional multi-word query (query *atheis**/*godless**/ nonbelie**) conducted via the search tools provided in the American Reference Library Database and within the "Supreme Court Decisions" collection it contains—which runs from an impressive 1793–1997 time span—returns 117 hits, all occurring from 1947 onwards. The first Supreme Court Decision referring to atheism is Everson v. Board of Education, 330 U.S. 1, 1947. This further confirms how much the focus on atheism seems to gain momentum with the early Cold War.
5. See for example "In Göttlicher Mission"—Der Kreuzzug des George W. Bush ("In Divine Mission": The Crusade of George W. Bush). Der Spiegel nr.8/2003 http://magazin.spiegel.de/EpubDelivery/spiegel/pdf/26383931 (Last consulted: August 29, 2018)
6. As apparent in Figure 2.3, Domke and Coe's corpus of Major Addresses (2008) contains no occurrence for *crusad** either. The only trace of Bush using *crusade* in relation to the 9/11 attacks that I have been able to find was through the same query *crusad** in the 1789–2009 Presidential Rhetoric corpus (10 hits in total: 6 hits for *crusades*, 3 hits for *crusade*, and 1 hit for *crusader*). Bush produced this occurrence while giving a speech to the troops at Elmendorf Air Force Base in Anchorage, Alaska (February 16, 2002). He said: "I want to thank the members of the Canadian Armed Forces who are here. I want to tell you something: We've got no better friends than Canada. They stand with us in this incredibly important crusade to defend freedom, this campaign to do

what is right for our children and our grandchildren." Only a few paragraphs later did he mention the fight against terror and 9/11. Wikipedia reports two more instances of a similar employ of the term *crusade* by G.W. Bush, i.e. in "a press conference upon arrival at the South Lawn of the White House, September 16, 2001", and in the National Day of Mourning held in the 9/11 attacks aftermath. (http://en.wikipedia.org/wiki/Tenth_Crusade Last consulted: December 31, 2017) Interestingly, the 6 occurrences of *crusades* produced by George W. Bush in our 1789–2009 Presidential Rhetoric corpus were all used to say that America's geopolitical actions had nothing to do with "the Crusades of a thousand years ago".

7. In his July 17, 1980 GOP Convention speech, Reagan's call to embark on a "national crusade to make America great again" acquired an unmistakable— and partially cold-war related—religious taste at the very end of the speech, when Reagan said:

> Can we doubt that only a divine providence placed this land, this island of free-dom, here as a refuge for all those people in the world who yearn to breathe freely: Jews and Christians enduring persecution behind the Iron Curtain, the boat people of Southeast Asia, of Cuba and of Haiti, the victims of drought and famine in Africa, the freedom fighters of Afghanistan and our own coun-trymen held in savage captivity? I'll confess that I've been a little afraid to suggest what I'm going to suggest. I'm more afraid not to. Can we begin our crusade joined together in a moment of silent prayer? God bless America.
>
> (Reagan, July 17, 1980. GOP Convention Speech)

8. Results based on the collocation patterns computed from the case-sensitive query *war on/war against* in the 1952–2008 PCS corpus.

9. The query *evil\** in the 1789–2009 Presidential Rhetoric corpus shows that George W. Bush is unique in his usage of the *evil* reference, at least when compared to all the other presidents covering the same post WWII era. The file assembled for the 2001–2009 Bush presidency is marked by an impres-sive 1,433 raw frequency, or 0.28 relative frequency per 1,000. Only Presi-dent Buchanan (1857–1861) and President Jackson (1829–1837) have higher scores (respectively 0.31 and 0.28 relative frequency scores). Interestingly, the reference to *evil\** is mostly a 19th-century phenomenon, and there is a clear declining—but never disappearing—pattern across time, although revived in no small amount—but in isolation—by George W. Bush. Interro-gating Domke and Coe's corpus of major presidential speeches (1933–2007) returns an even higher relative frequency for *evil\** in George W. Bush's major speeches file, i.e. 0.43. George W. Bush ranks highest and is then followed by F.D. Roosevelt (0.17), Truman (0.14), L.B. Johnson (0.09), and Clinton (0.07). Except for Carter who is totally absent here (and showed the lowest score in the 1789–2009 Presidential Rhetoric corpus), all the other presidents in Domke and Coe's corpus show a few references to *evil\**. The difference observed between the relative frequency of *evil\** in the Bush 2004 campaign speeches file (0.03) and the much higher relative frequencies observed in both presidential rhetoric corpora (0.28 in the 1789–2009 Presidential Rhetoric cor-pus and 0.43 in Domke and Coe's corpus) may seem quite intriguing. Also, it apparently casts some doubt on the results presented in Table 2.5 and on the quality of the Bush 2004 campaign speeches file. However, the dispersion plots returned from the query *evil\** in both presidential rhetoric corpora help reconcile the results of Table 2.5 with those returned from presidential rhetoric.

These dispersion plots (unreported in the present book) are made of bars, each one graphically accounting for one occurrence of the word and its location in the corpus file. Interestingly, the dispersion plots show that *evil\** mostly concentrates on the first half of both our 2001–2009 presidential corpus file and Domke and Coe's 2001–2007 corpus file. Even though impressionistic only and therefore not fully satisfactory, graphical evidence seems to suggest that our findings in Table 2.5 do not contradict the results from presidential rhetoric corpora. They indeed suggest that if Bush used many references to evil, these are at their most concentrated in the period prior to his 2004 campaign run. It does not seem unreasonable to posit that Bush's usage of the evil reference is the result of the 9/11 attacks.

10. The difference between the 1952 GOP file and the 1952 Democratic Party file is slightly significant ($X^2=6.91440$; difference is significant at p <0.01)
11. Some scholars have already started such comparative work. See for example Stramer 2012.

# References

Church, F. 2002. *The American Creed: A Biography of the Declaration of Independence*. New York: St. Martin's Griffin.

Church, F. 2007. *So Help Me God: The Founding Fathers and the First Great Battle Over Church and State*. Orlando, FL: Harcourt, Inc.

Domke, D. and Coe, K. 2008. *The God Strategy: How Religion Became a Political Weapon in America*. New York: Oxford University Press.

Eisenhower, D. 1948. *Crusade in Europe*. Garden City, NY: Doubleday.

Espinosa, G. (ed.). 2009. *Religion and the American Presidency: George Washington to George W. Bush*. New York: Columbia University Press.

Fath, S. 2004. *Dieu Bénisse l'Amérique: La Religion de la Maison-Blanche*. Paris: Seuil.

Gunn, T. J. 2009. *Spiritual Weapons: The Cold War and the Forging of an American National Religion*. Westport, CT: Praeger Publishers.

Hunter, J. D. 1991. *Culture Wars: The Struggle to Define America*. New York: Basic Books. Kindle eBook.

Inboden, W. 2008. *Religion and American Foreign Policy, 1945–1960: The Soul of Containment*. New York: Cambridge University Press. Kindle eBook.

Kirby, D. (ed.). 2003. *Religion and The Cold War*. New York: Palgrave Macmillan.

Lambert, F. 1997. "God—and a Religious President. . . [or] Jefferson and No God": Campaigning for a Voter-Imposed Religious Test in 1800. *Journal of Church and State*, Vol. 39, No. 4 (Autumn), 769–792.

Meacham, J. 2007. *American Gospel: God, The Founding Fathers, and The Making of a Nation*. New York: Random House.

Prothero, S. 2007. *Religious Literacy: What Every American Needs to Know—And Doesn't*. New York: HarperOne.

Reinhartz, A. 2013. *Bible and Cinema: An Introduction*. New York: Routledge.

Romanowski, W.D. 2017. English Cinema and the Bible. In Gutjahr, P. (ed.). *The Oxford Handbook of The Bible in America*. New York: Oxford University Press, 424–436.

Rozell, M. J. and Das Gupta, D. 2006. "The Values Votes"? Moral Issues in the 2004 Elections. In Green, J. C., Rozell, M. J. and Wilcox, C. (eds.). *The Values Campaign? The Christian Right and the 2004 Elections*. Washington, DC: Georgetown University Press, 11–21.

Shaw, T. 2003. Martyrs, Miracles and Martians: Religion and Cold War Cinematic Propaganda in the 1950s. In Kirby, D. (ed.). *Religion and The Cold War*. New York: Palgrave Macmillan.

Stramer, J. 2012. *U.S. Foreign Policy and Religion During the Cold War and the War on Terror: Study of How Harry S. Truman and George W. Bush Administrations Procured Public Support for Warfare*. The Edwin Mellen Press. http://mellenpress.com/mellenpress.cfm?bookid=8510&pc=9 Last consulted: May 16, 2014.

Swint, K. 2008. *Mudslingers: The Twenty-Five Dirtiest Political Campaigns of All Time*. New York: Union Square Press.

Vincent, A. 2014. *A Corpus Linguistics Approach to the Rhetorical God Gap in U.S. Presidential Campaigns*. Unpublished PhD thesis. Louvain-la-Neuve: Centre for English Corpus Linguistics, Université Catholique de Louvain.

# 3 The GOP's Rhetoric of Culture Wars and Anti-Liberalism

At the Republican Party National Convention of 1992, primary election candidate Buchanan proclaimed:

> This election is about much more than who gets what. It is about who we are. It is about what we believe, it is about what we stand for as Americans. There is a religious war going on in our country for the soul of America. It is a culture war, as critical to the kind of nation that we will one day be as was the Civil War itself.
>
> (Buchanan, 1992. GOP Party National Convention,
> quoted in Singh 2003: 1)

Although Buchanan's strong stance probably struck a chord with the audience and made history as "the culture war speech", it merely offered yet another version of a religiously charged storyline that had been told—and would keep being told—by other members of the GOP. In that story, the American identity had been conflated with the conservative agenda and pictured as endangered by several culture-war-related issues. As will be shown in the present chapter, this story has left several salient traces in our corpus of presidential campaign speeches.

There is general agreement that culture war issues such as abortion, stem cell research, gay rights, school prayers, creationism, religious displays in public places and the likes are of great concern to the religious conservative constituencies, which are said to be courted and won over through the GOP's insistence on these issues. The research reported in the present book returns several patterns that seem to confirm that such insistence in the campaign rhetoric of GOP candidates is real. However, it also demonstrates that several Democratic Party candidates did not beat a total retreat and tried to strike back in an effort to counter the conservative version of the culture war story. The overall picture that emerges from the present study is therefore that of a culture war battle led by the GOP, fought in words as well as in deeds, through different communication means and on different fronts.

The Republican Party's emphasis on the culture war issues is no legend, and a part of this emphasis has already been documented by Domke and Coe (2008: 99–128). In their study on religion in American politics, the authors highlight a "Morality Politics" gap (2008: 99)—taking shape around the 1970s–1980s—between the GOP and the Democratic Party. Domke and Coe's description of this morality politics gap is worth being quoted at length because it provides some important contextual information that should help us evaluate our own results and understand why they are linked to the entanglement of politics and religion:

> Religious conservatives believed that a moral revolution was needed. Such an outcome has been sought on a number of matters [like] school prayer, abortion, research on stem cells, the Equal Rights Amendment, and gay and lesbian relationships. These issues highlight church-state relations, origins of life, and sexual and gender norms, all of which have been central concerns of Christian conservatives since they politically mobilized. . . . The evidence will show that the GOP engaged in. . . *morality politics*, a form of public debate characterized by claims about what is right, good, and normal. Through their public communications, Republicans turned these issues into national, religious, and moral symbols. . . . [T]he Republican Party incorporated the core concerns of religious conservatives into the party's platform [and] elevated the gravity of issues such as abortion and same-sex relationships by calling for constitutional amendments and a reformed judiciary. Second, Republicans employed religious and moral language, a move that suggested that transcendent, "deeply held values" were at stake. . . . Morality politics, therefore, enabled the GOP to signal support for a key constituency's pet policies while providing a compelling justification that headed off criticisms of partisan pandering.
>
> (Domke and Coe 2008: 101–103)

In their chapter devoted to morality politics (2008: 99–128), Domke and Coe focus on the 1932–2004 national party platforms, which constitute a very appropriate source to investigate since they can be viewed as political manifestos containing the core values and main ideas defended by each party. However, because morality politics is defined as an electoral strategy to gain votes, failing to analyze the candidates' very own words in order to spot such a strategy limits the actual reach of Domke and Coe's observations. Because they directly derive from our analysis of campaign speeches, the patterns presented below supplement Domke and Coe's findings and offer a more refined picture.

## 3.1. Abortion, Stem Cell Research and Fetal Tissue Research

The abortion pattern reported in Table 3.1 parallels the morality politics strategy described in Domke and Coe (2008). It sets the modern-day GOP apart from its past and from the Democratic Party.

Reading the concordance lines containing the node *unborn* in the 1964 and 1968 Democratic Party files reveals no connection with the more recent culture war issue of abortion. By contrast, *abortion* (1996 GOP file) and *unborn* (2004 and 2008 GOP files) are culture-war related and are used to articulate the anti-abortion position of the GOP. In the case of *unborn* more specifically, it is used by George W. Bush to serve his call to defend "a culture of life".

This "culture of life" phrase calls for an enlightening digression. The word *culture* was found statistically significant in the Bush 2004 campaign speeches file in keyword analyses either opposing (1) Bush 2004 with Kerry 2004 (Log-Likelihood test score: LL67.44, p-value: 2.15–[14]) or (2) Bush 2004 with an aggregate wordlist of the 1980–1996 GOP files (Log-Likelihood test score: LL 137.62, p-value: 7.19–[16]). The keyword *culture* can thus be viewed as one specific signature of Bush's rhetoric as it sets him apart from his 2004 opponent as well as his Republican predecessors. A closer analysis of 2004 candidate Bush's usage of *culture* reveals that the term is almost exclusively connected to culture war issues. In a fashion that is quite typical of the culture war mindset, Bush defines the American culture as being at stake and endangered by what must be understood as the Hollywood liberal elitist leftist and un-American America, but protected on the other hand by the truly American communities:

> Most families do not look to Hollywood as a source of values. The heart and soul of America is found in caring communities like Toledo,

*Table 3.1* Abortion Pattern (Key keyword analysis, PCS corpus, rel. freq. per 1,000 words)

| Republican Party | Year | Democratic Party |
|---|---|---|
| – | from 1952 to 1960 | – |
| no 1964 GOP file | 1964 | unborn (0.03) |
| – | 1968 | unborn (0.08) |
| – | from 1972 to 1992 | – |
| abortion (0.16) | 1996 | – |
| unborn (0.03) | 2004 | – |
| unborn (0.02) | 2008 | – |

Ohio. . . . The direction of our **culture** is at stake. The decision is in the
best of hands. It's in the hands of the American people. It's in your hands.
(Bush, October 29, 2004. Campaign Remarks
in Ohio [emphasis mine])

Bush in turn expresses his desire to bend a "suspicious culture"[1] installed in
Washington—read the liberal side of Washington—by giving it a resolutely
more conservative curve. With Bush, *culture* appears as an umbrella term at
the service of the GOP's culture war agenda.

Also apparent in Bush's campaign rhetoric is the fact that *culture* can
endure quite a rhetorical contortion and serves as a very versatile tool at
the service of the GOP's agenda. Via his insistence on a "culture of responsibility", Bush attacks a Democratic Party-style Big Government, sells the
GOP's views on welfare and solidarity and defends his faith-based initia-
tive programme. It is interesting to note how—in Bush's 2004 campaign
rhetoric—religious dimensions gravitate around the GOP's social care
agenda, which mostly relies on individuals and nuclear institutions that are
not spurred into action by the government but by the moral responsibilities
that Bush does not fail to cloak in Golden-Rule-style religious language. In
his "Compassionate Conservative Agenda" speech (August 3, 2004, Dallas, Texas), Bush overtly expresses his belief that helping those in need
should mostly be left in the hands of those doing God's work every day.
Conflating religious conservative views with other aspects of the conservative agenda—notably those relating to welfare, solidarity or wealth
distribution—is the norm for GOP members. Quoting a 2011 Pew survey,
Jouet (2017: 175) for example explains that "the long-standing divide
between economic, pro-business conservatives and social conservatives
has blurred," and concludes that "[c]ontemporary American conservatives
commonly 'take extremely conservative positions on nearly all issues'".
Jouet adds that "this trend is likewise found among the public, as rank-and-
file conservatives have increasingly adopted hardline attitudes towards both
religion and economics since the 1980s" (2017: 178).

Commenting on the "culture of life" phrase is no vain digression, as it
relates to the abortion issue and the American culture wars discussed in the
present chapter. It also sheds some light on the Catholic Pattern that will be
discussed in Chapter 4. Interestingly, Gentile (2008) and Edsall (2006, qtd. in
Clermont 2009) explain that "culture of life" was borrowed from John Paul II
and used by Bush and his staff to specifically appeal to Catholic voters.

Table 3.2 below relates to another culture war issue, namely that of stem
cell research, and leans towards the Democratic Party side, although via the
2004 campaign file only.

Norrander and Norrander explain that "[a]rguments against stem cell
research often are intertwined with concerns over abortion. Both are elements of a 'culture of life' advocacy" (2007: 147). Table 3.1 indicates that the

*Table 3.2* Stem Pattern (Key keyword analysis, PCS corpus, rel. freq. per 1,000 words)

| Republican Party | Year | Democratic Party |
|---|---|---|
| no 1964 GOP file | from 1952 to 1996 | – |
| – | 2004 | stem (0.17) |
| – | 2008 | – |

abortion issue is statistically salient in the more recent Republican rhetoric. Table 3.2 shows that the related culture war issue of stem cell research is salient in the 2004 Democratic Party file. Interestingly, Norrander and Norrander highlight opinion poll evidence showing that a majority of American voters identified stem cell research "as being more strongly supported by Kerry and an issue on which more Americans favored Kerry over Bush" (2007: 150). Table 3.2 seems to suggest that such an assessment from American voters was correct indeed. Kerry's campaign file is the only one marked by a salient reference to the keyword *stem*. In every single case, the keyword *stem* is used by Kerry to talk about stem cell research. The query *stem cell\*/embryo\** returns no hit in the 1952–2008 GOP files. The same query in the 1952–2008 Democratic Party files (25 hits) shows that—even within his own party—Kerry is unique (22 hits returned for Kerry).[2] The only other instance that shows a reference to the stem cell research issue is to be found in the 2008 Obama file.[3]

The fact that the GOP candidates did apparently avoid the stem cell reference does not mean that the GOP has remained totally silent on stem cell research. Exploring concordance lines around the issue of abortion shows that GOP candidates resorted to umbrella terms—like "pro-life" (mostly Dole 1996) or "culture of life" (mostly Bush 2004)—through which their positions could be conveyed. In all likelihood, these umbrella terms served as catchphrases signalling to voters the Party's position on various culture war issues, stem cell research among them.

Running the same multi-word query (*stem cell\*/embryo\**) in the 1900–2008 National Party Platforms corpus reveals the GOP official—and pro-life—position on such an issue (with hits from 2000 onwards: *stem cell\**: 5 hits in the 2004 GOP platform and 3 hits in the 2008 GOP platform; *embryo\**: 1 hit in the 2000 GOP platform, 2 hits in the 2004 GOP platform, and 2 hits in the 2008 GOP platform):

Taxpayer-funded medical research must be based on sound science, with a focus on both prevention and treatment, and in accordance with the humane ethics of the Hippocratic Oath. In that regard, we call for a major expansion of support for the **stem-cell** research that now shows amazing promise and offers the greatest hope for scores of diseases— with adult **stem cells**, umbilical cord blood, and cells reprogrammed into pluripotent **stem cells**—without the destruction of **embryonic** human life. We call for a ban on human cloning and a ban on the creation of or experimentation on human **embryos** for research purposes.

(2008 GOP National Party Platform, emphasis mine)

One should not be misled by the GOP's officially expressed support for stem cell research. As Norrander and Norrander explain, there are various classes of stem cells, and "most controversy arises from the use of embryonic stem cells" (2007: 144). There is therefore no paradox in the GOP's apparent support for stem cell research, provided it does not use embryonic stem cells, which constitute the ethical line that many religious conservatives do not want to cross.

Another element indicates that the GOP has not been inactive in the stem cell research war. This piece of evidence is to be found in deeds more than in words, as the first bill ever vetoed by President George W. Bush concerned the so-called H.R. 810 Stem Cell Research Enhancement Act of 2005. Of this, Domke and Coe provide an enlightening description:

> Bush issued the first veto of his presidency. He had gone from January 2001 to July 2006 without vetoing a bill, the longest of any president since Thomas Jefferson. In breaking that string, the White House hosted a televised event in which Bush was surrounded by families with children born from frozen embryos.
>
> (Domke and Coe 2008: 135)

The July 2006 veto message returned by Bush to the House of Representatives[4] reads like another "culture of life" or "pro-life" manifesto.

In addition to expressing his opposition to Bush's ban on stem cell research (read embryonic stem cell research), Kerry linked such research to a culture war, arguing—in his campaign speeches—that through Bush, scientific progress had been killed on the altar of ideology. Although Kerry's rhetoric seems unique in its salient references to stem cell research, the national party platforms issued directly before and after his 2004 presidential bid leave little doubt as to the continuity of the Democratic Party's position in favour of embryonic stem cell research.[5] While the 2000 Democratic Party Convention issues a very short statement that "stem cell research [should be allowed] to make important new discoveries", the 2008 platform contains a longer note on stem cell research and against ideology-driven opposition to scientific progress:

> Research should be based on science, not ideology. . . . Yet, over the past eight years, the current Administration has not only failed to promote biomedical and **stem cell** research, it has actively stood in the way of that research. We cannot tolerate any further inaction or obstruction.

We need to invest in biomedical research and **stem cell** research, so that we are at the leading edge of prevention and treatment.

(2008 Democratic Party Platform [emphasis mine])

Democrats too turned words into deeds through President Obama's issuing Executive Order 13505—entitled "Removing Barriers to Responsible Scientific Research Involving Human Stem Cells" (March 9, 2009)—whereby "[t]he Presidential statement of August 9, 2001, limiting Federal funding for research involving human embryonic stem cells, shall have no further effect as a statement of governmental policy".

In order to spot other instances that potentially relate to the embryonic stem cell research, the query *stem cell\*/embryo\** was complemented by the nodes *fetal, foetal, foetus\** and *fetus\** and run in a larger set of corpora, i.e. the National Party Platforms corpus (1900–2008), the Presidential Campaign Speeches corpus (1952–2008) and the Campaign Ads corpus (1952–1996).[6] This query helped dig out several matches that relate to an older version of the stem cell research debate, to wit, the issue of fetal tissue research. In order to isolate this complementary batch of results from those already identified via the simpler *stem cell\*/embryo\** query run previously and analyze them with more ease, the query *stem cell\*/embryo\*/ fetal/fetus\*/foetal/foetus\** was then reduced to the two-word query *fetal/ fetus\** (as the query *foetal/foetus\** returned no hit). Corpus-wise, the query was narrowed down to the National Party Platforms corpus and the Presidential Campaign Speeches corpus since no hit for the query *stem cell\*/fetal/fetus\*/foetal/foetus\*/embryo\** was found in the 1952–2008 Campaign Ads corpus. With such new settings, the query returned 10 valid matches and revealed a gap in the communication means used by the Democratic Party and the GOP. As apparent in Figure 3.1, Democratic Party candidate Clinton exploited campaign speeches whereas the GOP preferred national party platforms to talk about fetal tissue research. Also apparent in Figure 3.1 is the fact that—while Kerry stands apart for his salient references to stem cell research in his 2004 campaign speeches (Table 3.2)—Clinton's campaign speeches are similarly unique in their references to fetal tissue research.

As one can observe in concordance line 10, Figure 3.1 (expanded here below), the oldest statement goes back to the 1976 GOP national platform and already contains pro-life tones:

While we support valid medical and biological research efforts which can produce life-saving results, we oppose any research on live fetuses. We are also opposed to any legislation which sanctions ending the life of any patient.

(GOP 1976 National Party Platform)

| N | Concordance | Set | File |
|---|---|---|---|
| 1 | of the Republican party who are anti-choice because of the fetal tissue research issue. That research opportunity offers us the | fetal | Clinton_Dem_1992.txt |
| 2 | bill was vetoed a few weeks ago by Mr. Bush because of the fetal tissue issue. And let me just say that bill had $300 million | fetal | Clinton_Dem_1992.txt |
| 3 | And he knows, my friend, a conservative businessperson, that fetal tissue research can do more to help solve the problems of | fetal | Clinton_Dem_1992.txt |
| 4 | the Women's Health Care Bill--caving in to the far right on the fetal tissue research--he threw away my son's best chance to | fetal | Clinton_Dem_1992.txt |
| 5 | of human embryos and against human cloning, the trafficking in fetal tissue organs, and related abuses. Academic Medical | fetal | Republican Platform of 2000.txt |
| 6 | outreach and education to expand public awareness. We call for fetal protection in biomedical research and will enforce the rights | fetal | Republican Platform of 1996.TXT |
| 7 | whose affects on women have yet to be determined. We call for fetal protection in the workplace and in scientific research. The | fetal | Republican Platform of 1992.TXT |
| 8 | mothers, especially the poor and young. We hail the way fetal medicine is revolutionizing care of children and dramatically | fetal | Republican Platform of 1988.TXT |
| 9 | our knowledge of human development. Accordingly, we call for fetal protection, both in the work place and in scientific research. | fetal | Republican Platform of 1988.TXT |
| 10 | can produce life-saving results, we oppose any research on live fetuses. We are also opposed to any legislation which sanctions | fetus* | Republican Platform of 1976.TXT |

*Figure 3.1* Query *fetal/fetus*\*(10 valid matches) in the 1900–2008 National Party Platforms corpus and in the 1952–2008 Presidential Campaign Speeches corpus

A quick search through the archives of the *New York Times* confirms that the issue of fetal tissue research connects to the culture war issue of abortion and to the divide separating the pro-choice and pro-life camps. In his 1992 paper "Bush Vetoes Bill to Lift Ban on Money for Fetal Research",[7] Clymer explains that "[t]he ban on use of tissue from abortions was imposed in 1988 by the Reagan Administration". The existence of such a ban confirms that there has been continuity in the GOP's positions relating to abortion, fetal tissue research and stem cell research.

As one can read in the two excerpts below, Clinton's 1992 campaign speeches—which are marked by a few references to fetal tissue research (Figure 3.1)—contain the same culture war tones. Note how—in the second excerpt—Clinton turns the "pro-life" label into a more negative "anti-choice" label to refer to the "far right" or else "most extreme elements" of the GOP. Of course, the Christian Right constitutes one of the main targets of the negative labelling employed by Clinton:

> I talked to a young businessman in Charlotte, North Carolina, a couple of weeks ago, who almost got tears in his eyes saying, "You know, I'm one of those people who's going to pay more taxes under your plan. But I've got a seventeen-year-old son, who's the most important person in the world to me. And he has diabetes. I want him to have a good life. And when George Bush vetoed the Women's Health Care Bill—caving in to the far right on the fetal tissue research—he threw away my son's best chance to have a normal life. I'm voting for a change this year. I want a change."
> (Clinton, October 22, 1992. University of Oregon speech)

> I was deeply dismayed when Mr. Bush vetoed the Women's Health Care Bill earlier this year, under pressure from the extreme elements of the Republican Party who are anti-choice because of the fetal tissue research issue. That research opportunity offers us the best chance that we have to deal with issues like diabetes. But the core of this administration's

| N | File | Words | Hits | per 1,000 | Dispersion Plot |
|---|------|-------|------|-----------|-----------------|
| 1 | Democratic Platform of 2000.txt stem cell* | 24,228 | | 0.04 | -0.069 |
| 2 | Democratic Platform of 2004.txt stem cell* | 17,803 | | 0.11 | -0.069 |
| 3 | Democratic Platform of 2004.txt embryo* | 17,803 | | 0.06 | -0.069 |
| 4 | Democratic Platform of 2008.txt stem cell* | 25,944 | | 0.12 | 0.250 |
| 5 | Democratic Platform of 2008.txt embryo* | 25,944 | | 0.04 | -0.069 |
| 6 | Republican Platform of 2000.txt embryo* | 34,672 | | 0.03 | -0.069 |
| 7 | Republican Platform of 2004.txt stem cell* | 41,399 | | 0.12 | -0.069 |
| 8 | Republican Platform of 2004.txt embryo* | 41,399 | | 0.05 | -0.069 |
| 9 | Republican Platform of 2008.txt stem cell* | 23,782 | | 0.13 | -0.069 |
| 10 | Republican Platform of 2008.txt embryo* | 23,782 | | 0.08 | -0.069 |

*Figure 3.2* Statistics returned from the query *stem cell\*/embryo\** in the National Party Platforms corpus (1900–2008)

> commitment to women's health was sadly lacking, and if elected on Tuesday, I will give that core back to American health policy.
>
> (Clinton, October 29, 1992. Justice Brennan Courthouse speech)

References to fetal tissue research are absent in the Democratic Party Platforms (Figure 3.1), but not the references to the more recent issue of stem cell research. As apparent in Figure 3.2, the Democratic Party has exploited its National Party platforms to articulate its views on stem cell research. However, Figure 3.2 also shows that the GOP returns—in aggregate—a slightly higher score in terms of raw frequencies for the multi-word query *stem cell\*/embryo\**:

The relative silence of a large majority of candidates but the clear positions expressed in National Party platforms and through Presidential actions, the use of umbrella terms like "pro-life" or "culture of life", the quite isolated case of Kerry 2004 and the additional hindsight provided by the older issue of fetal tissue research leave us in much of a quandary as to the kind of rhetorical gap—if any—we are observing here. Stem cell research is probably still too recent a phenomenon to be fully measured in rhetoric. Norrander and Norrander explain that candidates are apparently still hesitating about which position to adopt, but also say that "the fact that religious involvement is a dividing line on opinions about stem cell research—particularly among Catholics—suggests that stem cell research could become a new front in the 'culture war'" (2007: 159).

## 3.2. Family Values and Marriage

### 3.2.1. Family Values

The "family pattern" returned by our key keyword analysis and presented in Table 3.3 appears rather counterintuitive. According to Domke and Coe, the family theme should tilt the rhetorical God gap balance in favour of the

*Table 3.3* Family Pattern (Key keyword analysis, PCS corpus, rel. freq. per 1,000 words)

| Republican Party | Year | Democratic Party |
|---|---|---|
| – | from 1952 to 1960 | – |
| no 1964 GOP file | 1964 | families (0.27) |
| – | 1968 | families (0.21), family (0.65) |
| – | 1972 | families (0.33) |
| family (0.88) | 1976 | families (1.16), family (1.36) |
| families (1.07), family (1.12) | 1980 | families (0.83), family (0.75) |
| families (0.42), family's (0.11) | 1984 | families (0.37), family (0.80) |
| families (1.06), family (1.02) | 1988 | families (1.76), family (1.56) |
| families (0.54), family (0.94) | 1992 | families (0.37), family (0.90) |
| families (0.82), family (1.37) | 1996 | families (1.45), family (1.25) |
| families (1.24) | 2004 | families (1.69), family (0.72), family's (0.05) |
| families (0.73), family's (0.04) | 2008 | families (1.41), family (0.62), family's (0.06) |

1980s-onwards GOP (2008: 110–112). Amy Sullivan concurs and further notes that "the religious right [has] latched onto *'family values'*" (2008: 147). Such insistence on the family from the religious right is further evidenced by the existence of organizations like "Focus on the Family", the very name of which cannot be more explicit. Also, the organization's website[8] leaves little doubt as to its religious dimensions and is commonly described as "one of the most prominent [Christian Right] organizations" (Green et al. 2006: 7). Through the conservative prism, a word like *family* appears draped with a religious cloak. Given the consensus around the GOP's ownership of the family values thematic, Table 3.3 offers an unexpected picture.

In Table 3.3, the Democratic Party's focus on the family theme does not appear less important than in the Republican column. On the contrary, it spans a larger portion of the 1952–2008 timeline, and more or less parallels the relative frequency ebbs and flows observed for the GOP, but with relative frequencies that more than once score higher, not lower. However, Table 3.3 cannot be used as evidence against Domke and Coe's or Sullivan's observations. First, Domke, Coe and Sullivan imply that the GOP's insistence on the family theme is a specific signal to the religious conservatives. Table 3.3 does not provide any hint whatsoever regarding the various meanings— including the religious ones—that the family references acquire through the candidates' speeches. Despite quantitative appearances, the possibility exists that a semantic gap separates the way the family label has been resorted to by each party. Also, Domke and Coe's measure of the GOP's insistence on the family theme results from an approach that is different from our own. Theirs is based on a 1932–2004 party platforms corpus and on a multi-word query, including "all references to terms such as family, parents, marriage, wife, husband, and others of this kind" (2008: 110). For her part, Sullivan lays the focus on the more precise phrase "family values" (2008: 147). In his Dictionary of Religious Literacy—which contains a specific entry for "family values"—Prothero gives credence to Sullivan's more focused analysis:

> Family values. Although this term sounds ancient, it is actually of recent vintage, first used in its current sense in the late 1960s and injected into American cultural politics in the late 1970s. The Republican Party platforms of 1976 and 1980 endorsed "family values" as an antidote to what conservatives saw as the moral degradation of American society brought on by the sexual revolution, rock 'n' roll, and the counterculture. By the early 1980s this phrase . . . had come to serve as code for opposition to "atheistic schools, rampaging crime, God-forsaken homes, drugs, abortion, pornography, permissiveness and a sense of cynicism and spiritual desolation absolutely unprecedented in our country's history." . . . The term *family values* often serves as a proxy for "religious" in American political rhetoric. To be a family values candidate is to be a person of faith (and to appeal to conservative Christians).
>
> (Prothero 2007: 222–223)

Sullivan and Prothero's respective works imply that the gap between the GOP and the Democratic Party may be more easily revealed via specific phrases than via single words like those contained in Table 3.3. In doing so, both authors hint at an analytical shortcut to disambiguate the family pattern and reconcile Table 3.3 with a Republican tendency to tap into a religiously charged family language. As will become apparent next, such reconciliation will however not come without qualification elicited by some more counterintuitive findings.

Table 3.4 reports the results for the query *family value** across the 27 campaign speeches files. It is striking to note that these results confirm—rather than counterbalance—the counterintuitive pattern observed in Table 3.3. In Table 3.4, the GOP column is marked by a diachronic gap, and so is the Democratic Party column, although to a lesser extent. This diachronic gap seems to conform—at least to some degree—to the temporal location of what Domke and Coe call the "God Strategy", which they situate around Ronald Reagan's access to the White House (2008: 3). This diachronic gap echoing some scholarly findings notwithstanding, there is apparently not much of a quantitative gap separating—as one could have

*Table 3.4* Query *family value** in the 1952–2008 PCS corpus (rel. freq. per 1,000 words)

| Republican Party | Year | Democratic Party |
|---|---|---|
| no 1964 GOP file | from 1952 to 1964 | – |
| – | 1968 | family value* (0.002) |
| – | 1972 | – |
| – | 1976 | – |
| family value* (0.02) | 1980 | – |
| – | 1984 | family value* (0.06) |
| family value* (0.02) | 1988 | family value* (0.02) |
| family value* (0.08) | 1992 | family value* (0.14) |
| – | 1996 | family value* (0.02) |
| – | 2004 | family value* (0.02) |
| – | 2008 | family value* (0.006) |

otherwise expected—the GOP from the Democratic Party. On the contrary, the Democratic Party is actually marked by occurrences of *family value** that here again spread over a longer time span and that score higher in terms of relative frequencies. There are ebbs and flows in the relative frequencies observed, and both parties show a peak during the 1992 presidential campaign. The difference in relative frequencies—between both parties in the aggregate or between the 1992 campaign files more specifically—is not statistically significant.

Although the results presented in Tables 3.3 and 3.4 constitute an unexpected discovery, there is qualitative evidence confirming Domke, Coe and Sullivan's accounts. Diving into the campaign speeches through concordancing indicates that the difference is not so much about how frequently the Democratic Party candidates referred to *family value** as it is about what they actually said when using such a phrase. Figure 3.3 returns a selection of concordance lines (search node: *family value**) where the Democratic Party candidates themselves recognize—most of the time overtly—the GOP's specific insistence on family values which they in turn try to address.

As is apparent in Figure 3.3, most of the Democratic Party candidates who campaigned during a time identified by Domke, Coe, Sullivan and many other scholars as the era of the alliance between the GOP and the conservative religious right testified to the GOP's desire to own the "family values" issue. Table 3.4 indicates that the Democratic Party candidates talked about family values in no smaller amount than their GOP opponents, yet a share of this rhetoric was devoted to addressing the GOP's insistence on family values.

Concord

| File | Edit | View | Compute | Settings | Windows | Help |

| N | Concordance | File |
|---|---|---|
| 1 | I'm fed up with politicians in Washington lecturing the rest of us about "family values." Our families have values. But our government doesn't | Clinton_Dem_1992.txt |
| 2 | raise their kids, pay their taxes, play by the rules and embody those family values our adversaries spent so much time talking about in | Clinton_Dem_1992.txt |
| 3 | and neighbors as well. We've heard a lot of talk this year about family values, and that's fine with me: most of us wouldn't be here | Clinton_Dem_1992.txt |
| 4 | of our nation. I want an America that does more than talk about family values. I want an America that values families. I want an | Clinton_Dem_1992.txt |
| 5 | about honoring hard work, but worships the quick buck. It talks about family values, but doesn't value working families. How does Mr. Bush | Clinton_Dem_1992.txt |
| 6 | we will if you give me a chance to do it. Mr. Bush says he believes in family values. Well, I do, too. The difference is, I'm interested in your | Clinton_Dem_1992.txt |
| 7 | a while the "read my lips," education, environmental, kinder, gentler, family values president says this election is about trust. I ask you to | Clinton_Dem_1992.txt |
| 8 | has twice vetoed the family and medical leave bill, talking all about family values and then saying we can't do something that seventy-two | Clinton_Dem_1992.txt |
| 9 | the apple of his eye, has serious diabetes. They don't know why the family values president would veto a bill that would have invested this | Clinton_Dem_1992.txt |
| 10 | Four more years. Four more years of people who say they represent family values, but they increase the number of working poor, they | Clinton_Dem_1992.txt |
| 11 | nothing more important than that. George Bush likes to talk about family values. He talks about "a thousand points of light"; he talks | Dukakis_Dem_1988.txt |
| 12 | and the people we fight for. And it is time for those who talk about family values to start valuing families. [APPLAUSE] You don't value | Kerry_Dem_2004.txt |
| 13 | them less food, and more weapons. The Republicans say they're for family values. But families don't disown their weaker children. What | Mondale_Dem_1984.txt |
| 14 | than in Singapore. That's failure. The Republicans claim to stand for family values. But what family would disown its weaker children? | Mondale_Dem_1984.txt |
| 15 | For decades we've had politicians in Washington who talk about family values, but we haven't had policies that value families. Instead, | Obama_Dem_2008.txt |
| 16 | But while some politicians in Washington make a lot of noise about family values, when it comes to what people actually need to support | Obama_Dem_2008.txt |

*Figure 3.3* A selection of concordance lines for the two-word query *family value\** in the Democratic Party campaign speeches files

These testimonies from Democratic Party candidates themselves are surely informative, but they actually call for garnering quantitative evidence to confirm that such insistence on family values on the part of the Republican Party is actually real. Table 3.4 seems to suggest that, if it is the case that the family values gap is real, the GOP's insistence on family values is to be observed elsewhere than in general election speeches.

In what comes next, three additional sources are interrogated in order to see whether there is evidence that would make the family values gap quantitatively real. These sources are (1) our corpus of national party platforms for both parties, spanning from 1900 up to 2008, (2) our corpus of presidential rhetoric from President George Washington up to President George W. Bush (1789–2009) and (3) our corpus of campaign ads from 1952 up to 1996.

The results returned from the *family value\** query throughout the 1900–2008 National Party Platforms corpus highlight two gaps, i.e. a diachronic gap and a party gap. Contrary to Tables 3.3 and 3.4, Table 3.5[9] follows the patterns announced by scholarly research and denounced by several Democrats:

Figure 3.4 is a screenshot of all the concordance lines containing *family value\** (26 hits found in the 1900–2008 National Party Platforms corpus):

These lines are interesting on several counts. Lines 24 to 26 belong to the 1996 and 2008 Democratic Party platforms. They altogether officialise what Democratic Party candidates denounced in their campaign speeches, i.e. the Republican Party's insistence on family values. In turn, these two highly official Democratic Party manifestos lend further credence to the family values gap highlighted in scholarly research. Lines 1 to 23 all belong to the Republican Party platforms. One visible feature of these concordance lines is the fact that—through references to family values—the same message is hammered home again and again. Of course, one may retort that it is normal for a party to remain consistent with its core values from campaign to campaign. Yet Table 3.5 highlights a diachronic gap given that *family value\** is never

*Table 3.5* Query *family value\** in the 1900–2008 National Party Platforms corpus (rel. freq. per 1,000 words and raw freq.)

| Republican Party | Year | Democratic Party |
|---|---|---|
| – | From 1900 to 1972 | – |
| family value* (0.10, 2 hits) | 1976 | – |
| family value* (0.03, 1 hit) | 1980 | – |
| family value* (0.07, 2 hits) | 1984 | – |
| family value* (0.08, 3hits) | 1988 | – |
| family value* (0.25, 7 hits) | 1992 | – |
| family value* (0.07, 2 hits) | 1996 | family value* (0.11, 2 hits) |
| family value* (0.06, 2 hits) | 2000 | – |
| family value* (0.05, 2 hits) | 2004 | – |
| family value* (0.08, 2 hits) | 2008 | family value* (0.04, 1 hit) |

mentioned between 1900 and 1972. That such emphasis on *family value\** constitutes a singular addition to the traditional core values of the party therefore seems quite likely. Interestingly, such an addition is concomitant with the Christian Right's sudden focus on family values. Dowland explains:

> [T]he rise of the "family values" as the rallying cry of the Christian right was neither inevitable nor predictable. The triumvirate of political positions that came to constitute the core of "family values"—opposition to abortion, feminism, and gay rights—did not command much attention from evangelicals before 1975. . . . Over the course of the 1970s, however, a small cadre of evangelical ministers developed a political philosophy that connected defense of the "traditional family" with opposition to abortion, feminism, and gay rights. . . . [T]he genius of the movement was to frame opposition to abortion, feminism, and gay rights as "defense of the family." After all, who was going to argue against families? By the end of the 1970s, the Christian right had devised rhetoric that made liberal reformers enemies of the family and positioned "family values" as mainstream fare. Opposing abortion, feminism, and gay rights, in the view of the Christian right, would benefit *all* Americans.
>
> (Dowland 2009: 607–608)

Dowland then makes the link between the GOP agenda—which is officially defined in party platforms—and the Christian Right readily apparent when saying:

| N | Concordance | Se | File |
|---|---|---|---|
| 1 | their culture and land-tenure system, which fosters self-reliance and strong extended-family values. We support increased local self-government for the United | | Republican Platform of 2008.txt |
| 2 | which advocate it. We support the appointment of judges who respect traditional family values and the sanctity and dignity of innocent human life. We have made | | Republican Platform of 2008.txt |
| 3 | their culture and land-tenure system, which fosters self-reliance and strong extended-family values. We support increased local self-government for the United | | Republican Platform of 2004.txt |
| 4 | which advocate it. We support the appointment of judges who respect traditional family values and the sanctity of innocent human life. Our goal is to ensure that | | Republican Platform of 2004.txt |
| 5 | which advocate it. We support the appointment of judges who respect traditional family values and the sanctity of innocent human life. Our goal is to ensure that | | Republican Platform of 2000.txt |
| 6 | their culture and land-tenure system, which fosters self-reliance and strong extended-family values. We support increased local self-government for the United | | Republican Platform of 2000.txt |
| 7 | culture and land-tenure system, which fosters self-reliance and strong extended family values. We recognize that the people of Guam have voted for a closer | | Republican Platform of 1996.TXT |
| 8 | which advocate it. We support the appointment of judges who respect traditional family values and the sanctity of innocent human life. Our goal is to ensure that | | Republican Platform of 1996.TXT |
| 9 | cut off contributions to such organizations because of their courageous stand for family values. Moreover, we oppose efforts by the Democrat Party to include | | Republican Platform of 1992.TXT |
| 10 | the development of healthy, nurturing families. We applaud the fine example of family values and family virtue as lived by the President and the First Lady. We will | | Republican Platform of 1992.TXT |
| 11 | services. We reaffirm our support for appointment of judges who respect traditional family values and the sanctity of innocent human life. President Bush signed into | | Republican Platform of 1992.TXT |
| 12 | discipline. The Department of Defense will not be an exception to our assertion of family values. Republicans will not tolerate sexual harassment or misconduct | | Republican Platform of 1992.TXT |
| 13 | land tenure system which fosters self-reliance [c.51] and strong extended family values. When we lose farmers, we lose much more than agriculture. We are | | Republican Platform of 1992.TXT |
| 14 | in the fundamental goodness of the American people. We believe in traditional family values and in the Judeo-Christian heritage that informs our culture. We | | Republican Platform of 1992.TXT |
| 15 | of contemporary socialism under all its masks: to liberate youth from traditional family values by replacing family functions with bureaucratic social services. That | | Republican Platform of 1988.TXT |
| 16 | there is still much more to do. • We appointed judges who respect family rights, family values, and the rights of victims of crime. • We brought education back to | | Republican Platform of 1988.TXT |
| 17 | for the appointment of judges at all levels of the judiciary who respect traditional family values and the sanctity of innocent human life. • That churches, religious | | Republican Platform of 1988.TXT |
| 18 | committed to judicial restraint, the rights of law-abiding citizens, and traditional family values. We pledge to continue their record. Where appropriate, we support | | Republican Platform of 1988.TXT |
| 19 | federal judges committed to the rights of law-abiding citizens and traditional family values. We share the public's dissatisfaction with an elitist and | | Republican Platform of 1984.TXT |
| 20 | for the appointment of judges at all levels of the judiciary who respect traditional family values and the sanctity of innocent human life. [c.52] America Secure and | | Republican Platform of 1984.TXT |
| 21 | for the appointment of judges at all levels of the judiciary who respect traditional family values and the sanctity of innocent human life. Taxes and government | | Republican Platform of 1980.TXT |
| 22 | public scandal all create a hostile atmosphere that erodes family structures and family values. Thus it is imperative that our government's programs, actions, | | Republican Platform of 1976.TXT |
| 23 | we know that it is not powerful enough to replace them. Because of our concern for family values, we affirm our beliefs, stated elsewhere in this Platform, in many | | Republican Platform of 1976.TXT |
| 24 | global and a government that's gone AWOL. It's time we stop just talking about family values, and start pursuing policies that truly value families. We will expand | | Democratic Platform of 2008.txt |
| 25 | our families. The family is the foundation of American life. After 12 years of all family-values-talk and no family-values-action by the Republicans, President | | Democratic Platform of 1996.TXT |
| 26 | is the foundation of American life. After 12 years of all family-values-talk and no family-values-action by the Republicans, President Clinton took office determined | | Democratic Platform of 1996.TXT |

*Figure 3.4*   Concordance lines returned from the query *family value\** (26 hits) in the 1900–2008 National Party Platforms corpus

By convincing themselves that they represented a majority of Americans—and by convincing enough Americans that a liberal minority had launched a covert war on the family—Christian right leaders made "family values" an essential element in the Republican agenda.

(Dowland 2009: 631)

The messages around *family value\** are enduring and consistent, but only on a limited temporal portion that quite perfectly conforms to Domke and Coe's own findings. Diving more deeply into the concordance lines of Figure 3.4 confirms that *family value\** helps articulate a rhetoric that is religiously laden and oriented towards culture war issues. Worth noting is the recurrent insistence on the appointment of GOP-approved judges, which is a catch-all reference to culture war issues for which these judges are expected to fight "at all levels of the judiciary" (lines 17, 20 and 21, Figure 3.4). Such insistence relates to the judicial activism pattern that will be discussed in the third section of the present chapter. As will be explained in more detail, the rhetoric of the GOP is marked by the party's insistence on the appointment of conservative judges who would prevent activist judges from spreading their elitist, secular, liberal and leftist agenda which, the party believes, endangers the very nature of America itself.

The query *family value\** in our corpus of presidential rhetoric returns 382 hits located on the last 5 files of a corpus that spreads from George Washington to George W. Bush (Figure 3.5). Such dispersion on the 1789–2009 timeline brings further evidence for the diachronic gap previously

Concord

| File | Edit | View | Compute | Settings | Windows | Help |
|------|------|------|---------|----------|---------|------|

| N | File | Words | Hits | per 1,000 | Dispersion | Plot |
|---|------|-------|------|-----------|------------|------|
| 1 | 39 Carter James 1977 1981 TXT | 5,242,875 | 3 | | 0.478 | |
| 2 | 40 Reagan Ronald 1981 1989 TXT | 7,736,177 | 40 | | 0.810 | |
| 3 | 41 Bush George HW 1989 1993 TXT | 4,646,409 | 163 | 0.04 | 0.522 | |
| 4 | 42 Clinton William 1993 up to 1999 TXT | 11,801,170 | 138 | 0.01 | 0.481 | |
| 5 | 43 Bush GW 2001 2009 txt | 5,571,792 | 38 | | 0.608 | |

*Figure 3.5*  Distribution plots and statistics returned from the query *family value** in the 1789–2009 Presidential Rhetoric corpus

highlighted, but less so for a consistent quantitative gap separating the GOP from the Democratic Party.

Admittedly, the highest frequency scores are observed in the file of GOP President George H.W. Bush. Also, comparing the highest relative frequencies obtained by each party returns a significant difference between GOP President Bush and Democratic Party president Clinton ($G^2$=88.52366, difference is significant at p <0.001). However, Figure 3.5 indicates that—in presidential rhetoric—*family value** finds its origins not in the speeches of a Republican president, but in Carter's 1977–1981 presidential rhetoric.[10] Although the very low frequency observed in Carter's presidential speeches means that caution must be exercised, the presence of *family value** in his presidential rhetoric can probably be interpreted as a likely consequence of the 1976 campaign promise he made to evangelicals to support American families (Balmer 2008: 107; Dowland 2009: 606). Likewise, the fact that references to *family value** started in Carter's presidential rhetoric seems in sync with another easily forgotten fact, namely that the Christian Right experienced its political awakening by supporting Jimmy Carter before swinging to the Republican Party (see for example Balmer 2008: 79–107; Berlinerblau 2008: 10–11; Domke and Coe 2008: 13–17). As regards Carter's promise made to evangelicals to address the issue of family values, Balmer recounts:

> Carter, at least to some degree, played into the hands of the Religious Right. In the course of the 1976 campaign, he had promised to convene a White House conference that would address the concerns of families. Distracted by his other obligations however . . . Carter had placed the conference on hold. As the 1980 election approached, he felt obligated to redeem his promise and delegated the responsibility for organizing the conference to surrogates. When the White House Conference on Families opened in Baltimore on June 5, 1980, it became apparent that conference planners had taken a rather broad view of what constituted a family, including single-parent families and same-sex parents. Leaders of the Religious Right pounced on yet another reason to defeat the Southern Baptist incumbent. The term "family values" would become a mantra for religious conservatives in the years ahead.
>
> (Balmer 2008: 107)

Still in Figure 3.5, the fact that Clinton returns a higher relative frequency value than Reagan and George W. Bush—who are both conventionally depicted as experts of religious political language and champions of the Christian Right—strikes another quantitative blow against the theory of a one-sided Republican monopoly on family values references. Reading the concordance lines from President Clinton's rhetoric indicates that he tried to fight on the family values front by defining the GOP as the family values party in words only, while he defined the Democratic Party as the family values party in deeds.

Similarly to Domke and Coe—but via a more specific query across a larger National Party Platforms corpus—we have shown that a quite recent GOP-leaning family values gap is quantitatively and qualitatively apparent in the 1900–2008 National Party Platforms corpus. Another place where evidence for such a gap might be discovered is the Campaign Ads corpus (1952–1996). However, no such quantitative evidence was found there as the query *family value\** returned three hits only, i.e. 1 hit in a 1980 Carter campaign ad, 1 hit in a 1988 Bush campaign ad, and 1 hit in a 1992 Bush campaign ad. Such low raw frequencies do not bring any further quantitative support for the family value gap. Also, only the third ad mentioned (i.e. from the 1992 Bush campaign) returns an interesting and quite explicit illustration of how—in negative campaigning messages produced by the GOP—the reference to *family values* could acquire its religious dimensions and its connections to culture war issues. This 1992 Republican ad reads:

ANNOUNCER: Bill Clinton's vision for a better America includes job quotas for homosexuals, giving homosexuals special civil rights, allowing homosexuals in the Armed Forces. Al Gore supports homosexual couples adopting children and becoming foster parents. Is this your vision for a better America? For more information on traditional family values, contact the Christian Action Network.

Through an investigation of general campaign speeches and other sources of political discourse, we have found quantitative and qualitative evidence that the GOP has played a religiously charged family card. The evidence further suggests that Domke and Coe's findings as well as Sullivan's account are mostly correct. However, the evidence gathered here brings a more nuanced picture, where the Democratic Party does not appear totally absent on the family front. Despite the Democrats' efforts however, the GOP is still conventionally defined or perceived as owning the family values issue.[11] The contrast that exists between the quantity of family values talk produced by the Democratic Party and the perception that persists nonetheless that the GOP owns the family values issue will not be further explored in this book. However, two references in the literature (i.e. Nunberg 2006; Petrocik et al. 2003/2004) shed some interesting light on this contrast. Both seem to imply that, over the last few decades, the Democratic Party has been suffering from an issue ownership balance that has favoured the GOP and from the subsequent lack of opportunities to address issues that are not GOP-owned:

> It's only when you look at those patterns of usage that you discover how deep the Democrats' linguistic problems go. Over recent decades, the left has lost the battle for the language itself. When we talk about politics nowadays—and by 'we' I mean progressives and liberals as well as conservatives and people in the center—we can't help using language that embodies the worldview of the right. The challenge facing liberals and Democrats is to recapture that ordinary language.
>
> (Nunberg 2006: 4–5)

Later in his book, Nunberg offers another quite enlightening argument on the issue ownership gap and the distance there can be between the quantitative features of the rhetoric produced and the effects it has—or fails to have—on the audience's perception:

> That's what it means to say that the right owns *values*. Since the Nixon era, the word has been shorthand for a particular collection of narratives about the decline of cultural standards concerning sexuality, religion, hard work, and patriotism—anything they can bring up that's likely to make their "Middle Americans" angry about the drift of the culture. . . . The problem isn't just that the Democrat's value-talk smacks of defensive me-tooism, but that it betrays a certain semantic cluelessness. *Values* "works" for the right because it evokes the narratives that underlie its populist strategy. When conservatives present themselves as the defenders of values, they don't mean simply that their views are principled, but that they will uphold the views of "ordinary Americans" whose religious views and standards of personal morality have been mocked and traduced by out-of-touch elite liberals. *Values* is charged with the indignation and displaced class resentments that the right has been battening on for the last forty years. . . . Democrats don't really get this. They seem to assume that voters attach importance to "values" simply because they want to be reassured that a party's positions have a compelling moral basis. So they continue to talk about values as if the word could be purged of its populist connotations and restored to its old lexical purity as the bland synonym for moral principles that it was in the Eisenhower years. . . . In the absence of an alternative populist narrative, or for that matter any compelling narrative at all, the Democrats' invocations of "values" don't have the same power to stir moral indignation the way the word does in Republican mouths, where *values* is just another word for "morals".
>
> (Nunberg 2006: 107–109)

In a content analysis of presidential campaign ads and acceptance speeches produced from 1952 to 2000, Petrocik et al. highlight their discovery of a rather similar trend where the Democratic Party appears as actually helping to raise the saliency of the GOP agenda:

> Republicans were more focused than Democrats on the issues they owned. . . . Republicans put two-thirds or more of their efforts into issues owned by them. Democrats, by contrast . . . spent as much time raising Republican as Democratic issues. The net effect of the attention given to GOP issues is that slightly more than 60 of *all* the issues raised in acceptance speeches are GOP-owned and approximately 56 percent of all the issues raised in presidential campaign TV ads are GOP-owned. Put differently, Democrats did not balance off the Republican campaign effort. On the contrary, they effectively promoted a Republican agenda.
>
> (Petrocik et al. 2003/2004: 609)

Scholarly research on issue ownership seems to be in its infancy[12] and more evidence should probably be garnered to consolidate its early findings and to better measure how much a specific issue is owned by one or the other party. In all likelihood, corpus linguistics too could offer techniques that scholars like Petrocik et al. might be willing to consider in the future. No matter how much remains to be discovered, both Nunberg and Petrocik et al. highlight the fact that gaps can also materialize in issue ownership differences and in unequal receptions from the audience.

### 3.2.2. Marriage

In the conservative worldview, marriage is seen as the sacred union between a man and a woman. The advocates for such a strict and uncompromising definition hold that any other kind of marriage—and most notably gay marriage—poses a serious threat to the American family model and the very foundations upon which the American society rests. Table 3.6 indicates that the words *marriage* and *marry* were elements of choice in George W. Bush's campaign speeches.

*Table 3.6* Marriage Pattern (Key keyword analysis, PCS corpus, rel. freq. per 1,000 words)

| Republican Party | Year | Democratic Party |
| --- | --- | --- |
| no 1964 GOP file | from 1952 to 1996 | – |
| marriage (0.54), marry (0.13) | 2004 | – |
| – | 2008 | – |

Reading the concordance lines for Bush's employment of *marriage* makes the culture war subtext readily apparent and indicates that Bush used it to defend the conservative understanding of marriage. Consider these two excerpts:

> We stand for a culture of life in which every person matters and every being counts. We stand for **marriage** and family, which are the foundations of our society. We stand for the appointment of federal judges who know the difference between personal opinion and the strict interpretation of the law.
>
> (Bush, October 14, 2004. Campaign Remarks in
> Las Vegas [emphasis mine])

> The fifth choice in this election is on the values that are so crucial to keeping our family strong. And here, my opponent and I are miles apart. I believe **marriage** is a sacred commitment, a pillar of our civilization, and I will defend it. This is not a partisan issue. When Congress passed the Defense of **Marriage** Act, defining **marriage** as a union of a man and a woman, the vast majority of Democrats supported it. My predecessor, President Clinton, signed it into law. But Senator Kerry was part of an out-of-the-mainstream minority that voted against the Defense of **Marriage** Act.
>
> (Bush, October 23, 2004. Speech in Ft. Myers,
> FL [emphasis mine])

The keyword *marry* (Table 3.6) is used by George W. Bush to refer to his proposal to his then-to-be wife Laura. There is no apparent connection to culture war issues around the word *marry*, yet one may still suspect that behind such a salient usage of the word *marry* hides a potential desire to insist on the issue of marriage.

Given how important the defence of traditional marriage seems to be for the conservatives, one might have expected the keywords *marriage* and *marry* to be salient in other GOP campaigns, yet Table 3.6 indicates that only the Bush 2004 file is marked by both terms. Further investigations confirm that Bush—either as a candidate or as president—is quite specific and alone in his employment of the term *marriage*. The observed frequencies and relative frequencies (per 1,000 words) returned by the query *marriage* in the PCS corpus are quite striking: only 11 out of the 27 campaign files (5 GOP files, 6 Democratic Party files, 123 hits in total) contain at least one occurrence of the term *marriage*. Bush 2004 returns 98 hits and a relative frequency of 0.54. The second most frequent usage is found in Reagan 1984, with an astonishingly low relative frequency of 0.01 and only 3 hits. The same frequency analysis of the term *marriage* in the 1789–2009 presidential rhetoric corpus confirms that George W. Bush put the term *marriage* at the forefront of the culture war. The presidential speeches file for Bush (spanning from 2001 to 2009) returns 1,039 hits for *marriage*, with a relative frequency per 1,000 words of 0.19. The second highest relative frequency is found in Cleveland's presidential rhetoric (1885–1889), with a score of 0.03 (7 hits). Much chronologically closer to President Bush, his predecessor Clinton scores—in the same corpus of presidential rhetoric—100 hits and a much lower relative frequency of 0.008.

Bush's salient usage of *marriage* during his 2004 campaign and his presidency attests to the fact that the culture war on marriage was raging during the 2004 campaign and exploited by the Bush camp (see Wilcox et al. 2006: 56–75). Although idiosyncratically salient in terms of quantitative measures, Bush's usage of *marriage* is best understood as the culmination of a culture-war fight that was initiated over a decade earlier to protect the so-called traditional American family. This is illustrated in the 1992-onwards GOP platforms, which state:

> Republicans oppose and resist the efforts of the Democrat Party to redefine the traditional American family.
>
> (1992 GOP Party Platform)

> [W]e endorse the Defense of Marriage Act to prevent states from being forced to recognize same-sex unions. . . . [Congressional Republicans] passed the Defense of Marriage Act, which defines "marriage" for purposes of federal law as the legal union of one man and one woman and prevents federal judges and bureaucrats from forcing states to recognize other living arrangements as "marriages."
>
> (1996 GOP Party Platform)

> We support the traditional definition of "marriage" as the legal union of one man and one woman, and we believe that federal judges and bureaucrats should not force states to recognize other living arrangements as marriages.
>
> (2000 GOP Party Platform)

Wilcox et al. (2006: 56–75) and Wilcox and Robinson (2007: location 95–101 of 3980) highlight two important things about the issue of marriage and the 2004 campaign. First, one has to understand that this issue—probably like many other religiously laden culture war issues—gained momentum through various forces, not all of them being purely political. Politicians did clearly exploit culture war issues in an effort to gain votes, but probably in no small part because various religious groups considered them important and pressured politicians to take action (Wilcox and Robinson 2007: location 95 of 3980). Interestingly, this echoes Edwards's precious yet too often ignored advice to stop viewing political leaders as the sole and unique shapers of public opinion (2003: 74–75). Subsequently, it reminds us of the complexity of the American-style entanglement of religion and politics, and of how much focusing on actors other than politicians may bring an important contribution to a more complete understanding of this phenomenon. Second, Wilcox, Merolla and Beer also note that George W. Bush took position on the same-sex marriage issue quite hesitantly at first (2006: 59) and took precaution not to waste "political capital" by carefully devising "targeted communications with religious conservative voters" (2006: 60). They exemplify such targeted messages from the 2004 Bush campaign by explaining that "[t] he Republican National Committee mailed persuasion pieces in West Virginia and other states suggesting that liberals wanted to take away Bibles and allow same-sex marriage. It also ran ads on selected radio stations, which reach targeted audiences" (2006: 72). Likewise, they describe how "[c]arefully targeted phone messages reminded conservative voters that the future of marriage was at stake and that George Bush shared their values" (2006: 66). The authors further describe how Bush was careful not to embark on too strong religious stances, preferring instead to have "surrogates" (Ibid.) fight at the culture war forefront and "let the Christian Right groups debate same-sex marriage for him" (Ibid.). Yet for all his precautions, Bush's insistence on the marriage culture war issue still comes out from our key keyword analysis of general election speeches (Table 3.6). This second point levelled by Wilcox, Merolla and Beer teaches a lesson that is worth remembering. Because Bush is said to have resorted to surrogates to convey messages that were deemed politically risky, one must here again understand that the God gap may occur in rather specific—and probably low key—places. No matter how large the corpora used in this book are, there remain many other political actors to study, and many more places to explore.

## 3.3. Judicial Activism

Our key keyword analysis returned another pattern—made of the terms *justices*, *judges* and *judicial* (Table 3.7)[13]—that also connects to the American-style entanglement of religion and politics in general, and to the culture war issues in particular.

Anyone with an interest in the religious-political entanglement in America will sooner or later discover that the American way of religion cannot be fully grasped without consideration of the judicial branch and the many struggles and debates fought over in courts. Hunter reminds us that many a cultural or political divide has been fought in courts, as attested by 19th-century French political thinker De Tocqueville from whom Hunter quotes: "[T]here is hardly a political question in the United States which does not sooner or later turn into a judicial one" (De Tocqueville, qtd. in Hunter 1991: Location 3261 of 5465). Hunter is nonetheless quick to add that such a state of

*Table 3.7* Judicial Pattern (Key keyword analysis, PCS corpus, rel. freq. per 1,000 words)

| Republican Party | Year | Democratic Party |
|---|---|---|
| no 1964 GOP file | From 1952 to 1968 | – |
| judges (0.15) | 1972 | – |
| – | 1976 | – |
| – | 1980 | judges (0.12) |
| – | 1984 | justices (0.14) |
| judges (0.17) | 1988 | – |
| – | 1992 | – |
| judges (0.21) | 1996 | – |
| judges (0.15) | 2004 | – |
| judges (0.21), judicial (0.18), justices (0.03) | 2008 | – |

affairs "is undoubtedly more true now than in the 1830s", and that the courts have occupied a centre-stage position in the more recent culture wars (Ibid.). Hunter further explains that the evolving culture wars are fought through "court packing" (location 3270–3278 of 5465), which is a strategy that aims at gaining significant influence by placing the "right" judges at all levels of the judiciary. Hunter's explanations are quite enlightening:

> The most conspicuous area over which the legal system is contested is in the composition of the bench itself—judges selected by the president as federal court appointments. This is no small affair, for as history makes clear, judges not only decree what the Constitution legally requires, but what it morally implies as well. The power of selection vested in the executive branch of the government, therefore, is nothing less than a temptation to prejudice the bench in favor of those judges and attorneys whose legal philosophy and opinions are most compatible with the current administration.
>
> (Hunter 1991: Location 3270 of 5465)

In their more recent study (2008), Domke and Coe explain that the religious conservatives have been quite angry at court decisions and in turn willing to stop and reverse—notably through court packing—what they take as liberal, elitist, anti-religious and anti-American forces that have sneaked their way into the judicial branch. Domke and Coe explain:

> In most cases, [religious conservative] voters sought the passage of new laws and the installation of new judges to uphold them. The former

without the latter was viewed as inadequate: after all, it was the justices of the U.S. Supreme Court who banned school prayer, legalized abortion, and legitimized same-sex relationships. Consequently, the contempt felt by many religious conservatives for the judiciary is raw. . . . This anger at the courts has not dissipated, and it often peaks when a seat on the Supreme Court becomes available.

(Domke and Coe 2008: 102)

The opinion of Family Research Council president Tony Perkins—whom Domke and Coe cite—deserves being quoted at length as it captures and encapsulates many of the religious conservatives' grievances against the judicial branch:

Whether it was the legalization of abortion, the banning of school prayer, the expulsion of the 10 Commandments from public spaces, or the starvation of Terri Schiavo, decisions by the courts have not only changed our nation's course, but even led to the taking of human lives . . . For years activist courts, aided by liberal interest groups like the ACLU, have been quietly working under the veil of the judiciary, like thieves in the night, to rob us of our Christian heritage and our religious freedoms. Federal judges have systematically grabbed power, usurping the constitutional authority that resides in the other two branches of government and, ultimately, in the American people.

(Perkins 2005 as qtd. in Domke and Coe 2008: 102–103)

In their analysis of party platforms, Domke and Coe have identified—on the GOP side—an increase in the number of references to the Constitution and the judiciary that is concomitant with the growing religious political entanglement of the 1980s:

[F]rom 1932 through 1976 Republicans and Democrats referenced the U.S. Constitution and the judiciary in almost identical amounts in their platforms. . . . With the rise of religious politics in 1980, however, the Constitution and the judiciary became symbols of national morality, with the GOP issuing platform calls for amendments to institute voluntary prayer in public schools, to end legal abortion, and to prohibit same-sex marriage. The result is that from 1980 through 2004 the GOP roughly tripled the Democrats in platform references to both the Constitution and the judiciary. Further, additional analysis shows that the parties diverged in even greater degree in the past few elections. In platforms 1996–2004, Republicans more than quadrupled Democrats in emphases on the Constitution and the courts. There is such synchronicity in the platform language because the GOP has consistently paired

calls for constitutional amendments with criticisms of Court decisions
and judicial ideologies.

(Domke and Coe 2008: 108–109)

Interestingly, our key keyword analysis of presidential campaign speeches
suggests a rather similar—and complementary—pattern. As one can read in
Table 3.7, there is a fairly recent and GOP-leaning insistence on *judges, judicial* and *justices*. This time and party gap more or less parallels Domke and
Coe's and Hunter's descriptions, with two notable exceptions—to wit, the
1980 and 1984 Democratic Party campaigns—which are the ones that contain
salient references to *judges* (1980) and *justices* (1984). If these results do not
totally contradict Domke and Coe's findings quoted earlier, they at least have
the merit of putting things into better perspective and illustrate once more
that cut-and-dried polarities do not necessarily best describe what differen-
tiates the GOP from the Democratic Party. Parenthetically, it is interesting
to note that searching for the terms *judge/judges/constitution/supreme court/
judiciary* in the 1980 campaign speeches for both Reagan (GOP) and Carter
(Democratic Party) returns results that go counter to the expectations elicited
by Domke and Coe's research. In aggregate, Carter produced 82 occurrences
of these terms (rel. freq. per 1,000 = 0.42), whereas Reagan produced 6 hits
only (rel. freq. per 1,000 = 0.06). The search terms *constitution* and *supreme
court* are for example mentioned more frequently by Carter (23 hits and 12
hits respectively) than by Reagan (2 hits and 3 hits respectively). The 1980
and 1984 campaigns aside, the rest of the results contained in Table 3.7 confirm that the GOP's campaign rhetoric is characterized by its insistence on the
judiciary and its attacks against activist judges.

Querying *judges/justices/judicial* in the GOP campaign speeches files
where these nodes were found significant (i.e. in 1972, 1988, 1996, 2004 and
2008, see Table 3.7) returns results that connect to Hunter's and Domke and
Coe's research. A mere look at the collocation patterns[14] (Figure 3.6) is enough
to understand that through their insistence on the nodes *judges/justices/judi-
cial*, most if not all of these GOP candidates discussed the appointments of
conservative judges who strictly or faithfully interpret the constitution, unlike
the so-called liberal and activist judges who—in the GOP candidates' views
at least—legislate from the bench and are guilty of judicial activism.

The statistics returned for these GOP candidates (Figure 3.7) indicate
that quantitative differences exist nonetheless, with the highest cumulative
relative frequency[15] being obtained by Dole (1996) and even more so by
McCain (2008).

Also, reading the concordance lines for the GOP 1972 campaign speeches
file indicates that Nixon's rhetoric mostly focused on criminality and too
permissive judges rather than on judicial activism on the part of liberal and
elitist judges. Nixon's usage of the node *judges* does not echo the religious

| N | L5 | L4 | L3 | L2 | L1 | Centre | R1 | R2 | R3 | R4 | R5 |
|---|----|----|----|----|----|--------|----|----|----|----|-----|
| 1 | FOR | THE | APPOINTMENT | OF | FEDERAL | JUDGES | WHO | THE | THE | DIFFERENCE | BETWEEN |
| 2 | TO | TO | WE | STAND | OF | JUDICIAL | TO | KNOW | AND | THE | THE |
| 3 | AND | APPOINT | THE | WILL | APPOINT | JUSTICES | POWER | WILL | TO | AND | TO |
| 4 | THE | AND | I | AND | FOR | | OF | HAVE | INTERPRET | THAT | AND |
| 5 | WILL | APPLAUSE | AND | TO | THE | | AND | AND | WILL | TO | OF |
| 6 | HAVE | OF | | BY | LIBERAL | | ACTIVISM | ARE | | CONSTITUTION | LAW |
| 7 | OF | A | | WE | AND | | WE | A | | FAITHFULLY | INTERPRET |
| 8 | | | | APPOINT | CONSERVATIVE | | IN | FAITHFULLY | | | |
| 9 | | | | SUPREME | ACTIVIST | | | STRICTLY | | | |
| 10 | | | | THE | COURT | | | | | | |

*Figure 3.6* Collocation patterns for the nodes *judges/judicial/justices* in the 1972, 1988, 1996, 2004 and 2008 GOP campaign speeches files (L5 R5 search span; min. frequency of collocate: 5; stop at sentence break; sorting: raw frequency values)

| N | File | Words | Hits | per 1,000 | Dispersion | Plot |
|---|------|-------|------|-----------|------------|------|
| 1 | Dole_GOP_1996.txt judges | 184,373 | 39 | 0.21 | 0.657 | |
| 2 | McCain_GOP_2008.txt judges | 276,619 | 57 | 0.21 | 0.631 | |
| 3 | Bush_GOP_1988.txt judges | 83,105 | 14 | 0.17 | 0.528 | |
| 4 | Bush_GOP_2004.txt judges | 182,352 | 28 | 0.15 | 0.859 | |
| 5 | Nixon_GOP_1972.txt judges | 110,124 | 16 | 0.15 | 0.774 | |
| 6 | McCain_GOP_2008.txt judicial | 276,619 | 33 | 0.12 | 0.454 | |
| 7 | McCain_GOP_2008.txt justices | 276,619 | 8 | 0.03 | 0.650 | |
| 8 | Bush_GOP_1988.txt judicial | 83,105 | 2 | 0.02 | 0.300 | |
| 9 | Bush_GOP_1988.txt justices | 83,105 | 1 | 0.01 | -0.069 | |
| 10 | Bush_GOP_2004.txt judicial | 182,352 | 2 | 0.01 | 0.300 | |
| 11 | Dole_GOP_1996.txt judicial | 184,373 | 2 | 0.01 | 0.300 | |
| 12 | Dole_GOP_1996.txt justices | 184,373 | 2 | 0.01 | -0.069 | |

*Figure 3.7* Statistics returned from the query *judges/judicial/justices* in the 1972, 1988, 1996, 2004 and 2008 GOP campaign speeches files

conservatives' anger at the courts and does not apparently relate to the contextual background provided by Hunter and Domke and Coe. In turn, it means that Nixon's rhetoric constitutes an exception to the collocation patterns presented in Figure 3.6, although his insistence on "tougher" judges who must protect the victims rather than the criminals is to be found in his successors' rhetoric as well.

Reading through the 204 concordance lines returned from the query *judges/justices/judicial* and diving even deeper into source texts indicate that the GOP candidates coming after Nixon (i.e. in 1988, 1996, 2004 and 2008) produced a rhetoric which—in spite of quantitative differences observed in Figure 3.7—remains quite stable and coherent in its accusations of judicial activism and in its charges against liberal judges who are said to legislate from the bench.

As regards the very label "activist judges" or variations thereof, the query *activist jud\*/judicial activis\** through the 27 files of the PCS corpus (11 hits) leaves no doubt as to the fact that these labels are part of a name-calling strategy employed by a few Republican presidential candidates. No hit was found in the Democratic Party files (Figures 3.8 and 3.9)

| N | Concordance | File |
|---|---|---|
| 1 | appoint doctrinaire liberals. That's what he did in Massachusetts. But the excessive judicial activism of the '60s and '70s is one reason Americans turned against that | Bush_GOP_1988.txt |
| 2 | working with the Knights to defend the sacred bond of marriage. (Applause.) A few activist judges have taken it upon themselves to redefine the institution of marriage | Bush_GOP_2004.txt |
| 3 | an honored place in our society. I support the protection of marriage against activist judges. And I will continue to appoint federal judges who know the difference | Bush_GOP_2004.txt |
| 4 | how we fail to fulfil our constitutional responsibilities when we write laws that invite judicial activism and misinterpretation. Why these restraints on Federal judges? | McCain_GOP_2008.txt |
| 5 | of constitutional discourse. these abuses by the courts fall under the heading of "judicial activism." But real activism in our country is democratic. Real activists seek | McCain_GOP_2008.txt |
| 6 | often shown great idealism and done great good. By contrast, activist lawyers and activist judges follow a different method. They want to be spared the inconvenience | McCain_GOP_2008.txt |
| 7 | and the depth and breadth of one's empathy." These vague words attempt to justify judicial activism – come to think of it, they sound like an activist judge wrote them | McCain_GOP_2008.txt |
| 8 | words attempt to justify judicial activism – come to think of it, they sound like an activist judge wrote them. And whatever they mean exactly, somehow Senator | McCain_GOP_2008.txt |
| 9 | Samuel Alito. Apparently, nobody quite fits the bill except for an elite group of activist judges. lawyers, and law professors who think they know wisdom when they | McCain_GOP_2008.txt |
| 10 | to check the abuses of other branches of government if it cannot control its own judicial activism. Real activists seek to make their case democratically – to win | McCain_GOP_2008.txt |
| 11 | often shown great idealism and done great good. By contrast, activist lawyers and activist judges follow a different method. They want to be spared the inconvenience | McCain_GOP_2008.txt |

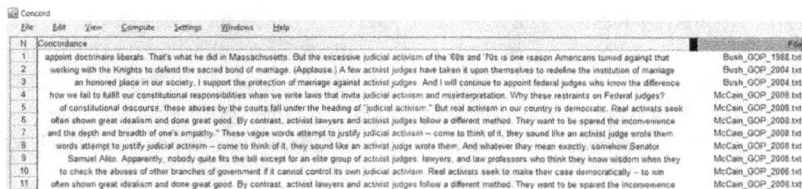

*Figure 3.8* Concordance lines returned from the query *activist jud\*/judicial activis\** in the 1952–2008 Presidential Campaign Speeches corpus (11 hits)

| N | File | Words | Hits | per 1,000 | Dispersion | Plot |
|---|---|---|---|---|---|---|
| 1 | Bush_GOP_1988.txt judicial activis* | 83,105 | 1 | 0.01 | -0.069 | |
| 2 | Bush_GOP_2004.txt activist jud* | 182,352 | 2 | 0.01 | 0.300 | |
| 3 | McCain_GOP_2008.txt activist jud* | 276,619 | 4 | 0.01 | 0.192 | |
| 4 | McCain_GOP_2008.txt judicial activis* | 276,619 | 4 | 0.01 | 0.429 | |

*Figure 3.9* Statistics returned from the query *activist jud\*/judicial activis\** in the 1952–2008 Presidential Campaign Speeches corpus

The GOP's attacks against judicial activism are also to be observed outside campaign speeches. According to Domke and Coe's measures (2008: 108–109), such attacks have integrated the 1980–2004 GOP platforms. A keyness analysis opposing the 2000–2008 party platforms of both parties indicates that a word like *activist* remains a keyword in the more recent 2000–2008 GOP platform aggregate file (LL8.32, p value 0.003, collocating with *judges* in every case). Diving deeper into the source texts confirms that the 2008 GOP platform is no exception to the now quite traditional "anti-activist judges" language that Domke and Coe observe in the 1980–2004 GOP platforms. In their study of 2004 mail pieces, Monson and Oliphant show that the activist-judges-bashing strategy—which both authors identify as an exploitation of religion for political gain—occurred in microtargeted (i.e. not broadcast) messages as well (2007: 111–112).

As mentioned earlier, the 1980 (Carter) and 1984 (Mondale) Democratic Party files are also marked by a salient reference to either *judges* (in 1980) or else to *justices* (in 1984) in Table 3.7. Carter's references to *judges* are interesting for several reasons. For one, Carter overtly recognizes the lifelong influence a president may exert through the nominations of judges. In his October 3, 1980 Address to the National Association of Women Judges, Carter could not have been clearer when stating: "Few things that a president does will have as much long-term effect as the judges that are appointed". On several occasions through the campaign, Carter repeated the same opinion that "[the president's] actions echo down through the years in the judges he appoints" (Carter, October 29 and 31, 1980, remarks at a rally with Area Residents). A second element in Carter's usage of *judges* that is quite enlightening is that he denounces—and therefore recognizes the existence of—an ideological court packing strategy. Although Carter remains rather vague as to the real identity of the "groups" he criticizes, it does not take a political science genius to understand whom he refers to when saying:

> I'm concerned . . . that some groups around this country are attempting to set up ideological eligibility tests for judges. . . . It's a radical departure from what all previous presidents, Democratic or Republican, have done. And as long as I'm president, potential judges will not be subjected to tests of religion or gender or race or personal beliefs on someone's list of so-called "right" attitudes.
>
> (Carter, October 3, 1980. Address to the National
> Association of Women Judges)

Among the plausible explanations for Carter's vagueness, one seems quite likely. In his presidential run in 1976, Carter received the support of many evangelical Christians (see for example Balmer 2008: 79–80). Consequently, one might posit that while running for re-election in 1980, Carter was quite keen to avoid alienating his supporters among the religious conservatives by pointing fingers at specific groups. Such vagueness more or less vanished however when it came to pointing fingers at politicians, as Carter did not hesitate to overtly accuse his GOP opponent of trying to imprint an ideological bent on the judiciary:

> I'd like to outline for you a few key basic issues that separate me from my Republican opponent. On one side, you've got a Republican candidate who promises ideological loyalty tests for possible federal judges, including members of the Supreme Court. On the other side, you've got a Democratic administration pledged to an independent qualified judiciary.
>
> (Carter, October 31, 1980. Remarks at a
> rally with area residents)

In his October 3, 1980 address to the National Association of Women Judges, Carter makes his critique even more resonant—and the contrast with his opponents starker—by pushing the ethical bar quite high for himself. Carter stated:

> I would be honored to be the first president to appoint a woman to the Supreme Court, but I cannot make such a promise. I can promise,

based on my record so far, that women and members of minority groups will be fully considered, but I will not rule out anyone—male or female—on the basis of sex or race or religion or national origin. To do that, to me, to promise ahead of time that I would comply with your wish, would violate the principles for which you and I have both fought so hard and would violate the trust that's been placed in me as president.

(Carter, October 3, 1980. Address to the National Association of Women Judges)

However, even Carter could be found guilty of double standards, as at other times, he used his own potentially milder yet no less real version of the court packing strategy in order to appeal to minorities. At the September 26, 1980 Hispanic Democratic Victory Dinner, Carter said:[16]

I have quadrupled already the number of Hispanic federal judges, including the first Hispanic woman federal judge, Carmen Consuelo Cerezo. And this, as you know, will have a major impact on the attitude and tone, not only in the court itself but in the entire communities where they serve, not just during my term of office, no matter whether it's four or eight years, but for a long time, for a generation.

(Carter, September 26, 1980. Hispanic Democratic Victory Dinner)

Similarly—this time addressing African-Americans instead of a Hispanic audience—Carter boasted:

I've appointed twice as many black judges as all the other presidents put together in the history of this country. But that's not enough.

(Carter, October 23, 1980. White House Reception for Black Ministers)

In a speech delivered at the 37th Tri-Annual Convention of the International Ladies Garment Workers Union, Carter stated:

Equal pay for equal work is a standard that ILG set a long time ago. It's the time now that the rest of the country caught up with you. Women make up 43 percent of the work force; a fourth of American households are headed by women—more and more American families depend on the wages that women bring home. When we help women to achieve greater economic rights, we are helping the American family. That's why we must put muscle behind our anti-discrimination laws, why we've toughened the Equal Employment Opportunity Commission,

why I personally have appointed more women to top federal positions
and more women judges to the federal bench than all previous presidents in the 200-year history of our nation combined.

(Carter, September 29, 1980. Address at the 37th Tri-Annual
Convention of the International Ladies Garment
Workers Union)

Worth noting is the fact that Carter defines the appointment of women judges
as being part of his strategy to support the so-called (and still unpassed) Equal
Rights Amendment (ERA), which constitutes another issue of the culture wars
opposing liberal proponents to conservative opponents. Among the reasons
explaining the conservatives' opposition to such an amendment, Hunter identifies the fear of seeing—here again—the traditional family model shattered, or
even the belief that such an amendment would constitute a stealth attempt to
"[smuggle] legal protection of homosexual rights into a Constitutional amendment" (Hunter 1991: location 2368 of 5465). Interestingly, we can read in the
excerpt above how Carter plays the family card too to defend the ERA, arguing
that helping women means helping the American family.

From these excerpts, we understand that court packing is a strategy
that Carter apparently understood as well as denounced yet employed and
boasted about to appeal to minorities and to fight on the culture wars front.
Interestingly, the 1980 campaign speeches file of his opponent Reagan is
not marked by a salient usage of any of the words in Table 3.7, and nor is
the Reagan 1984 file. In spite of the intriguing paradox posed by Carter's
critique of Reagan and Reagan's non-salient usage of the nodes *judges/judi-
cial/justices*, we will not dig deeper here into the reasons that could explain
Reagan's relative silence.

As for 1984 Democratic Party candidate Mondale, his salient usage of
the node *justices* is directly connected to the culture wars issues and the
Christian Right. Reading the concordance lines returned from the multi-
word query *judges/judicial/justices* in the 1984 Democratic Party file (22
matches) indicates that Mondale is—as opposed to Carter—everything but
vague when denouncing the influence of Rev. Jerry Falwell—and therefore
of the Christian Right—on the selection of the Supreme Court Justices.

Interestingly, our main key keyword analysis returned *falwell* and
*falwells* as idiosyncratically salient in Mondale's 1984 campaign file.
Looking for overt references to the Christian Right like these (Rev.
Jerry Falwell being one of its most prominent members) and analyzing
the kind of rhetoric produced around them falls beyond our scope. What
can already been observed from running the query *falwell/falwells/moral
majority/christian right* in the 1952–2008 PCS corpus and reading the 30
concordance lines returned[17] is that Mondale's overt references to—and
attacks against—Rev. Jerry Falwell and the Christian Right seem to be his
specific signature.

## 3.4. The GOP's Anti-Liberal Rhetoric

In 2006, UC Berkley Professor Nunberg authored a book with a rather catchy title, viz. *Talking Right: How Conservatives Turned Liberalism Into a Tax-Raising, Latte-Drinking, Sushi-Eating, Volvo-Driving, New York Times-Reading, Body-Piercing, Hollywood-Loving, Left-Wing Freak Show.* If—as the saying goes—a picture is worth a thousand words, then there is little doubt that Nunberg's very picturesque title offered the second-best option to capture the imagination and create a visual—and quite funny— representation of "the liberals" when seen through the conservative prism.

As will become apparent below, our analyses point towards a quantitative and qualitative evolution of the term *liberal* (and its inflected forms) and confirm a GOP-organized deriding of liberalism as well as the abandonment of the term by the Democrats. Our research also indicates that Nunberg's title could actually be made even longer and amended with culture-war-related— and religiously charged—terms like, *inter alia*, pro-abortion, pro-gay marriage and constitutional revisionists. This in turn echoes the description made by Jouet of what it means to be a conservative in America and how this definition has recently evolved into an uncompromising one-size-fits-all form of conservatism. According to Jouet, being conservative increasingly implies going for the full package and endorsing conservatism in all its varied forms, be they related to social and culture-war-related issues, the role of the government, or fiscal and economic issues (Jouet 2017: 175–178). The GOP-led attacks against liberalism have mirrored the same trend and have been launched across the board and on several fronts, resulting in a closely woven web of intertwined issues meant to negatively charge liberalism and turn it into a bad word. Through the Republican prism, liberalism appears as a pervasive force endangering virtually every aspect of the only true—read conservative—American way of life and the very fabric of the nation itself.

Such a trend is probably still unfolding, as attested—although tentatively—by a cursory collocation network analysis run on the most recent corpus I have been able to build so far. This corpus contains all the primary debates held during the 2016 presidential campaign (513,646 words, both parties).[18] Figure 3.10 presents a collocation network graph around the node *liberal\** (wildcard activated, 60 hits)[19] computed on the basis of a subcorpus comprising the 2016 Republican primary debates (12 prime-time debates and 7 undercard debates, 356,097 running words), and generated via the Lancs-Box GraphColl program (version 4.0) (Brezina et al. 2015). Table 3.8 reports the settings used to compute the collocation network graph following the Collocation Parameters Notation (CPN) proposed by Brezina et al. (*Ibid.*).

In order to ease the interpretation of Figure 3.10, a few complementary explanations are quoted from LancsBox's user guide[20] in the frame below. Please note that these explanations are mere excerpts from far more complete and detailed explanations provided on LancsBox's companion website.

*Table 3.8* Settings applied for the computation of the GraphColl-generated collocation network around the node *liberal\** in the 2016 GOP primary debates
subcorpus

| Statistic ID | Statistic name | Statistic cut-off value | L and R span | Minimum collocate freq. (C) | Minimum collocation freq. (NC) | Filter: Collocate, not |
|---|---|---|---|---|---|---|
| 03 | MI | 9.5 | L5-R5 | 1 | 1 | /bushes\|galston\| quote,"one\|nina\| turner\|somewhat\| ram\|throat\| william\|writing\| tip\|downtrodden\| grabbing\|proudly\| donated\|normally\| o'neill\|responded\| claimed\|1950s\| evolved\|heartless\| version\|400/ |

03-MI (9.5), L5-R5, C1-NC1 filter applied (Filter: Collocate, not)

---

A collocation network is an extended collocation graph that shows
i) shared collocates and ii) cross-associations between several nodes.

A collocation network displays nodes with unique collocates (outer
rim of the graph) and shared collocates (middle of the graph). The links
between nodes and shared collocates are indicated by a dash-dot line.

Position: the collocates are dispersed evenly around the node with
a 'L' or 'R' index displayed above the collocate circle indicating their
original position to the left and to the right respectively.

Strength: The strength of collocation as measured by the association measure is indicated by the distance (length of line) between the
node and the collocates. The closer the collocate is to the node, the
stronger the association between the node and the collocate ('magnet
effect').

Frequency: Collocation frequency is indicated by the intensity of
the colour of the collocate. The darker the shade of colour, the more
frequent the collocation is.

Source: Excerpts from LancsBox's user guide (version 3.0), http://corpora.
lancs.ac.uk/lancsbox/help.php Last consulted: October 22, 2018.

As explained in Brezina et al.:

> any discourse rests upon a large network of associations, where each
> one activates a number of others (cf. Hoey 2005), that produces social
> meaning through multiple cross-associations. These cross-associations,
> however, cannot be observed even with careful reading of source docu-
> ments, but need to be analysed using a tool that allows simultaneous
> multiple comparisons of word frequencies and co-occurrences. *Graph-
> Coll* . . . is a tool designed specifically for this type of research.
>
> (2015: 155)

As suggested above by Brezina et al. and explained in Hoey's lexical priming theory to which they refer, "[a word] becomes cumulatively loaded with
the contexts and co-texts in which it is encountered, and our knowledge of
it includes the fact that it co-occurs with certain other words in certain kinds
of context" (Hoey 2005: 8). In the present collocation network analysis of
*liberal\**, it is therefore not the collocates in isolation that interest us as such,
but rather their cumulative effect on *liberal\** and the GOP-induced meaning
that results from it. Following this rationale—and because the subcorpus
analyzed is rather small in size and therefore more prone to contain collocations with lower raw frequencies than a larger corpus—the choice was
made to allow for even the rarest collocates and collocations to be identified
(see collocation frequency and collocate frequency values in Table 3.8) if
showing a statistically strong association with *liberal\**.

As apparent in Figure 3.10, five direct collocates of the node *liberal\**
were expanded—to wit, *five-justice*,[21] *medicaid-expanding*, *far-left*, *elite*
and *pro-abortion*—and their respective collocates generated accordingly.
All these collocations (between *liberal\** and its five expanded collocates)
are—in our small subcorpus—unique in terms of frequency (each occurring
only once) but it is quite easy to see how these rare instances all contribute
to the same uncompromising interpretation of the term *liberal*. Figure 3.10
also identifies—via labels added to the screenshot from GraphColl—the
candidates who generated these associations with *liberal\**. The subcorpus is
too small to allow any kind of definite conclusion, yet it is interesting to see
that Trump is absent from Figure 3.10, contrary to the expectations one may
have built on the back of the expanded collocate *elite*—produced by candidate Fiorina—and its association with the media, which Trump is known
to have criticized quite frequently and violently. Future research could help
better evaluate how Trump's language has followed or else differed from a
more traditional form of conservative discourse. Likewise, candidate Cruz
seems to stand out for his anti-liberal pro-conservative rhetoric (also see
Figure 3.11 below), and more research could help better evaluate how much

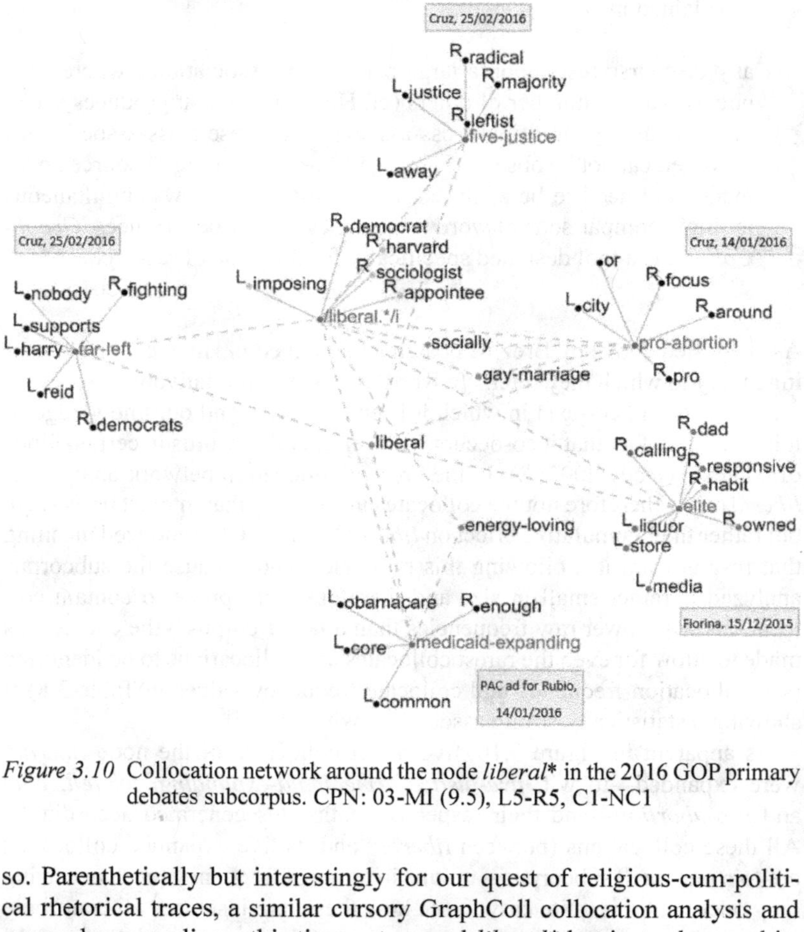

*Figure 3.10*  Collocation network around the node *liberal\** in the 2016 GOP primary
debates subcorpus. CPN: 03-MI (9.5), L5-R5, C1-NC1

so. Parenthetically but interestingly for our quest of religious-cum-political rhetorical traces, a similar cursory GraphColl collocation analysis and
concordance reading—this time not around *liberal\** but instead around its
counterpart *conservative\** (same subcorpus used, same settings,[22] wildcard
activated, 208 hits in total, 157 hits for *conservative*, 51 hits for *conservatives*)—return an interesting pattern where candidate Cruz explicitly associates conservatives with evangelicals and links conservatism to the defence
of Judeo-Christian principles (Figure 3.11).

Through the shared collocates and cross-associations that it reveals, the
extended collocation graph presented in Figure 3.10 gives an enlightening graphical sense of how *liberal\** is negatively charged and attacked on
several intertwined fronts, most of which are directly related to culture war
issues mentioned earlier in this chapter, and a few significant others being
connected to issues like healthcare, social services and the dangers posed by
elitist and socialist impulses from "the far left". From Figure 3.10, one gets

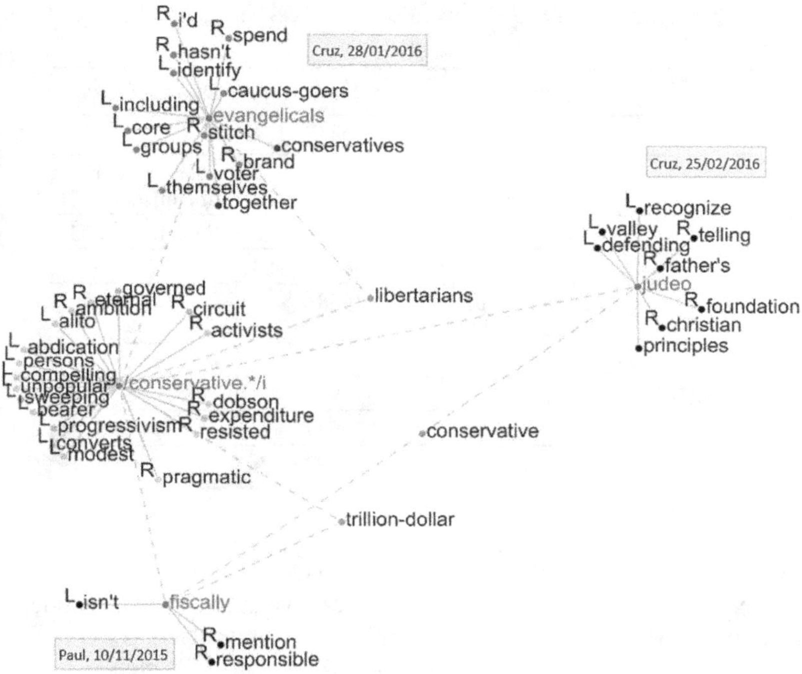

*Figure 3.11* Collocation network around the node *conservative\** in the 2016 GOP primary debates subcorpus. CPN: 03-MI (9.5), L5-R5, C1-NC1

the sense that—through the Republican prism—the word *liberal* activates concerns about judicial activism, implies being part of the far-left and the elite and involves certain culture-war-related stances like the support for abortion and gay-marriage (*gay-marriage* is a shared collocate of *liberal* and *pro-abortion*). As will be demonstrated in the remainder of Section 3.4, the liberal-bashing arsenal observed in Figure 3.10 is not of recent vintage but instead stems from the abandonment of the term *liberal* by the Democrats around the early 1970s and the subsequent recuperation thereof by the GOP, which has from then on spared no effort to turn *liberal* into a negatively charged word. In what follows, we return to our main key keyword analysis of the PCS corpus in order to analyze what it helped reveal about the word *liberal* and its inflected forms.

As apparent in Table 3.9, an interesting pattern takes shape when sorting the key keywords *liberal/liberals/liberalism* according to the time and party variables.[23]

There is a rather uncontroversial consensus about the fact that the Democratic Party is more liberal and the GOP more conservative (see for example

*Table 3.9* Liberal Pattern (Key keyword analysis, PCS corpus, rel. freq. per 1,000 words)

| Republican Party | Year | Democratic Party |
|---|---|---|
| – | 1952 | – |
| – | 1956 | liberal (0.25), liberalism (0.08) |
| – | 1960 | liberalism (0.03) |
| no 1964 GOP file | from 1964 to 1984 | – |
| liberal (0.46), liberalism (0.10), liberals (0.13) | 1988 | – |
| liberal (0.22), liberals (0.13) | 1992 | – |
| liberal (0.77), liberals (0.11) | 1996 | – |
| liberal (0.14) | 2004 | – |
| – | 2008 | – |

Singh 2003: 13). One might therefore be struck to see that—albeit salient in the 1950s and 1960s Democratic Party campaign speeches—the liberal references apparently left the Democratic Party vernacular and were recuperated by the 1988–2004 conservative GOP. Figure 3.12 plots a similar pattern based on the wildcard query *liberal\** in the entire 1952–2008 Presidential Campaign Speeches corpus.[24]

As documented in Vincent (2014: 200–205), a similar trend is observed in both the 1952–1996 Campaign Ads corpus and the 1900–2008 Party Platforms corpus. Put together, our corpora therefore reveal a rather good picture of how the liberal references have evolved—or better said, nearly vanished—quantitatively in the Democratic Party campaign rhetoric. But we still remain rather clueless as to their qualitative evolution. Diving deeper into the PCS corpus and conducting a qualitative analysis of its source texts returns a more complete picture of this liberal pattern. As will become apparent in the ensuing analysis, the liberal references have gone through a radical and upside-down evolution, combining a sharp decrease in frequency with a qualitative "turn on their heads".

The concordance lines that can be generated from the key keywords in Table 3.9 are too numerous[25] to be exhaustively accounted for in this book. However, concordance reading indicates that these concordance lines boil down to only a few different messages. Table 3.10 has been compiled for the purpose of illustrating how the "liberal" references have been used through time and by each party. To make the qualitative analysis through time more thorough, Table 3.10 contains excerpts from Eisenhower's 1956 and Clinton's 1996 campaign files, although Table 3.9 shows no salient "liberal"

**liberal\* in the 1952-2008 Presidential Campaign Speeches corpus**

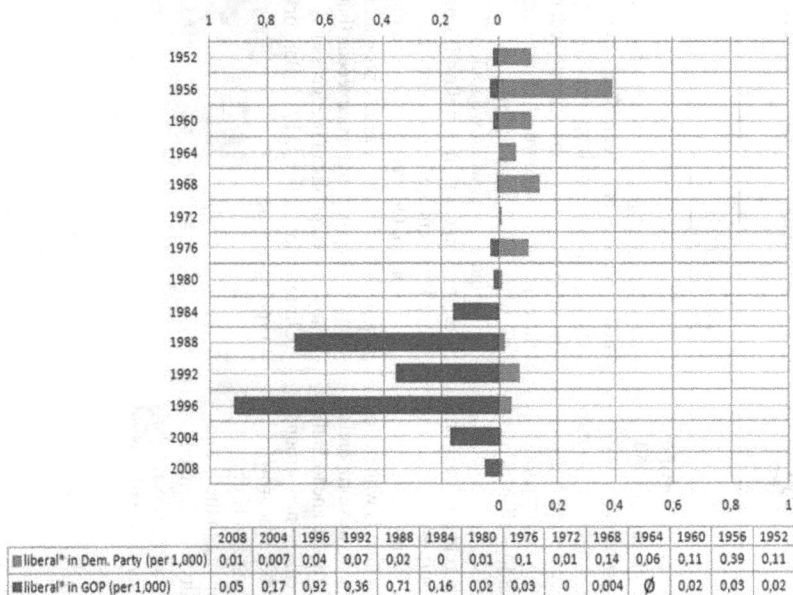

| | 2008 | 2004 | 1996 | 1992 | 1988 | 1984 | 1980 | 1976 | 1972 | 1968 | 1964 | 1960 | 1956 | 1952 |
|---|---|---|---|---|---|---|---|---|---|---|---|---|---|---|
| liberal* in Dem. Party (per 1,000) | 0,01 | 0,007 | 0,04 | 0,07 | 0,02 | 0 | 0,01 | 0,1 | 0,01 | 0,14 | 0,06 | 0,11 | 0,39 | 0,11 |
| liberal* in GOP (per 1,000) | 0,05 | 0,17 | 0,92 | 0,36 | 0,71 | 0,16 | 0,02 | 0,03 | 0 | 0,004 | Ø | 0,02 | 0,03 | 0,02 |

*Figure 3.12  liberal\** in the 1952–2008 Presidential Campaign Speeches corpus (rel. freq. per 1,000 words)

keywords for these campaigns. Before moving to the analysis proper, the reader is encouraged to carefully read Table 3.10 and consider these samples across time, across party lines, or else by comparing the "extremes" (e.g. Clinton 1996; Eisenhower 1956; Dole 1996; Stevenson 1956).

Let us first begin with the Democratic Party, which returns the oldest occurrences of the salient keywords *liberal* and *liberalism* in 1956 and 1960 (see Table 3.9). In Table 3.10, we can see quite plainly that Stevenson (1956) and Kennedy (1960) were far from shying away from the label "liberal". On the contrary, they seemed quite happy to endorse it. Interestingly, both accepted the nomination of the Liberal Party of New York Convention[26] in addition to their nomination at the Democratic Party Convention. While addressing the Liberal party of New York Convention, Stevenson and Kennedy both recognized that liberalism and the Liberal Party of New York had already been the source of attacks from the other side. Both addressed these attacks in rather enlightening ways. As we can read in Table 3.10, Stevenson for example said that the liberals at the receiving end of the GOP-organized liberal bashing should actually be proud of such

*Table 3.10* Rhetorical evolution of liberal/liberals/liberalism in the Democratic Party campaign speeches and in the GOP campaign speeches: source text excerpts from the PCS corpus.

| Stevenson 1956 (D) | Kennedy 1960 (D) | Clinton 1996 (D) |
|---|---|---|
| All of us here tonight call ourselves Liberals, whether with a large or a small "L." . . . You of the Liberal party have been subjected to the charge that you are idealists. I hope you rejoice in the accusation, and that you will always prove worthy of it. . . . Surely this is a time for idealists . . . It is in this spirit that I accept your nomination tonight. (Stevenson, September 11, 1956, Speech at the Liberal Party of New York Convention, acceptance of Liberal Party Nomination) | I accept your nomination, and I am proud of it. I am proud to be the only candidate in 1960 with the nomination of two political parties . . . I do not regard the title of liberal as an honorary degree; I regard it as a license to preach the gospel of liberalism across this country. . . . I believe for these reasons that liberalism is our best and our only hope in the world today. . . . Only liberalism, in short, can repair our national power, restore our national purpose, and liberate our national energies. And the only basic issue in the 1960 presidential campaign is whether our government will fall in a conservative rut and die there, or whether we will move ahead in the liberal spirit of daring, of breaking new ground, of doing in our generation what Woodrow Wilson and Franklin Roosevelt and Harry Truman and Adlai Stevenson did in their time of influence and responsibility. . . . (Kennedy, September 14, 1960, Speech at the Liberal Party of New York Convention, acceptance of Liberal Party Nomination) | Let me tell you what this is not. This is not about liberal and conservative. Our administration has the most fiscally conservative record in modern history. We're the first administration to reduce the deficit in all four years of our term in the twentieth century. It is now 63 percent lower than it was when we took office. Our government is the smallest it's been since President Kennedy came here to campaign. Our record in abolishing regulations and unnecessary programs and privatizing programs exceeds that of my two Republican predecessors. (Clinton, November 4, 1996, Bangor Airport Speech) |

| Eisenhower 1956 (GOP) | Bush 1988–1992 (GOP) | Dole 1996 (GOP) |
|---|---|---|
| And I want, here, to pay tribute to your two senators from this state—Senator Hickenlooper and Senator Martin. They have been leaders in what I call Republicanism adjusted to the conditions of modern life. They are _progressive_ Republicans. (Eisenhower, September 1956, Remarks to Republican Leaders and Precinct Workers and A Group of Newspaper Editors) This administration has acted to help the family farm in the most concrete ways: social security for farm operators; the federal gas tax refund; the Soil Bank; the most _liberal_ Farm Credit Program in history; the biggest, most creative research program to find new products, new uses for old products, new markets for all products. (Eisenhower, October 10, 1956, Remarks at Centennial Plaza) | We have strived hard these last eight years to put some balance and common sense back in the courtroom, but it is my great concern that my opponent would reverse that trend and send us right back to the days of _liberalism_ and ultra-leniency in our courts. This is why I feel it my duty to draw the distinctions between me and my opponent as sharply and clearly as possible, so that the American people can make their decision. Because in a very real sense, the election this November is about more than the next four years, it will define the nature of our courts for a generation to come. As president, I will appoint judges who understand that it is their job to interpret the law, not legislate from the bench. I spoke earlier of a _liberal_ ideology that will push ahead with its social experimentation despite the cost. Today I've tried to show how this ideology has shaped—or misshaped—our criminal justice system. At other times, I've spoken about how it applies to other issues, such as taxes and spending, the size of government, and the national defense. That's what this election comes down to—two fundamentally opposed visions of America and where we want to lead her. (Bush, October 7, 1988, Xenia Law Enforcement Community Speech) | [Y]ou know President Clinton doesn't like that word "_liberal_." I mean, every time I mention it, he'd . . . [missing text] . . . "don't tell anybody. Don't tell anybody. I want to keep it a secret until after the election." You're going to hear it every day, Mr. President. You're going to hear it every day because you are a _liberal_, Mr. President. You are a _liberal_. You ought to be proud of it. . . [missing text] . . . you're a _liberal_. But he's . . . doesn't want anybody to know it, doesn't want you to see it. (Dole, October 7, 1996, Milltown Speech) So, I want to conclude this, and remind you of two or three, I think, basic things, that sometimes I wonder if people are focusing on. . . . I want to protect the flag that's being waved out here today with a Constitutional amendment. I want to protect the flag. And he's against it. I believe we can have voluntary prayer in school and he's against it. That's the basic difference. And I will appoint conservative judges to the bench who will interpret the Constitution. And if you send me a partial birth abortion bill I will sign it; I will not veto it. . . . I'm |

*(Continued)*

Table 3.10 (Continued)

| Eisenhower 1956 (GOP) | Bush 1988–1992 (GOP) | Dole 1996 (GOP) |
|---|---|---|
| | Governor Clinton and Congress don't want kids to have the option of praying in school, but I do. Clinton and Congress don't want to close legal loopholes and keep criminals behind bars, but I will. Clinton and Congress will stock the judiciary with liberal judges who write laws they can't get approved by the voters. (Bush, July 20, 1992, GOP National Convention Acceptance Speech)<br><br>I'll give you another reason to reelect me. I think we've got a great first lady in Barbara Bush, I'll tell you. When she holds those AIDS babies in her arms or when she reads to those children or when she lifts up these families, she's saying, "Family values do matter." Don't let the liberals and the media tell you they don't. They do matter. God bless the American families. (Bush, November 2, 1992, Remarks at the Briarcliff Father and Son Athletic Association) | a conservative; he's a liberal. Don't let him fool you. For the first—he's already had two terms. He had one two-year term where he was a liberal. Now, the last two years he's trying to act like a moderate or something else. . . . This is the real candidate Clinton, not the candidate who's out there now talking like a conservative. Keep this in mind. He's never changed. He's a liberal. He's a liberal. He's a liberal. Don't let him forget it. (Dole, October 23, 1996, Speech in Macon) |

accusations. Not included in Table 3.10 but worth mentioning nonetheless are other passages of the same speech where Stevenson derides his opponent (i.e. President Eisenhower), the Eisenhower administration as well as the GOP, for being anti-intellectuals trying to rebuild the image of the GOP by welcoming a few intellectuals—whom Stevenson ironically congratulates for having not only read a book but also written one—and by trying to reframe the Party's image as "progressive" and "liberal".[27] Interestingly, we can read in Table 3.10 how Eisenhower did indeed tap into the language of liberalism and progressivism. Still in the same speech (but again not apparent in Table 3.10), Stevenson explains that the Republican Party is inextricably linked to big business, property and wealth and therefore incapable of exercising the proper functions of government and the executive branch. The only valid alternative left is liberalism and the Democratic Party.

As one can read in Table 3.10, Kennedy too took much pride in being labelled a liberal despite the anti-liberalism attacks from the other side. In terms that sound more radical than those employed by Stevenson, Kennedy summarized the stakes of the campaign to a rather simple conservative/liberal dichotomy with only one possible choice, that of liberalism, unless one would be ready to see the government "fall in a conservative rut and die". From both Stevenson and Kennedy, we understand that attacks against liberalism were already present, yet these Democratic Party candidates did not shy away from being tagged "liberal". On the contrary, they were actually quite willing to contrast conservatism with liberalism and exploited their own version of the liberal/conservative divide at a time when—as we can understand from Eisenhower's sampled speech—"liberal" and "progressive" could still convey positive meanings.

Yet the proud liberalism of old would soon be replaced by the Democratic Party's retreat on the conservative/liberal rhetorical front. Clinton's boasting about his administration's most fiscally conservative record in modern history and his reducing the government more drastically than even his GOP predecessors (see third column of Table 3.10) speaks volumes about the upside down evolution undergone by the liberal references in the Democratic Party rhetoric. Contrary to Stevenson and Kennedy, Clinton avoids the liberal/conservative dichotomy.

On the other side of the political spectrum, we can read how Dole tapped into the conservative/liberal divide and depicted liberalism as something to be ashamed of. Also of interest are the culture war issues gravitating around the liberal/conservative rhetoric produced by Dole. In another speech not quoted in Table 3.10 (i.e. Dole, October 10, 1996. "Ohio Bus Tour Kick-Off"), Dole echoed Stevenson and Kennedy when suggesting that the elections came down to a binary choice between "stealth liberals"—which is a label found in Dole's campaign speeches file only—and "common-sense conservatives". Dole then added a promise that he honoured indeed, i.e.

"They don't want you to know they're liberal, but I'm going to tell you every time I get a chance that they're liberal" (Ibid.).

As indicated in Table 3.9, the 1988 and 1992 GOP campaigns are also marked by the liberal key keywords. Table 3.10 contains three enlightening samples. In the first one, 1988 GOP candidate Bush articulates his views around liberalism by defining it as an ideology of a hopefully bygone age, the pervasive influence of which has created much damage already and will continue to do so should the electoral outcomes favour the Democratic Party. The stakes awaiting Americans are therefore high, yet the choice is quite simply put between a dangerous liberal ideology and Bush's conservatism. Still in the first sample, we can read how Bush connects liberalism to the issue of court packing (see Section 3, Chapter 3). The second sample shows that in 1992, Bush still associates liberalism with court packing and the judiciary. Also of interest are the issues of school prayer and criminality gravitating around Bush's discussing the liberal word. In the third sample, Bush puts "the liberals" and "the media" under the same umbrella and points an accusing finger at their deriding the family values that we discussed earlier.

If we could picture the liberal/conservative tension as a long-lived theatrical play, we could say that—somewhere around the 1980s—the roles were quite clearly inverted on the rhetorical stage, while some actors—on the right of the political spectrum—grew much more vocal in the process.[28] Consider how similar Stevenson and Dole appear in their deriding their opponent for being—respectively—a conservative or a liberal in disguise. The rhetoric produced by both Eisenhower and Clinton gives at least some credit to their accusations. Once proudly endorsed by Stevenson and Kennedy, the tag "liberal" grew into something of a bad word that only Dole—not Clinton—was still willing to associate with the Democratic Party.

As Table 3.9 indicates, the 2004 GOP file is also marked by the key keyword *liberal*. The concordance lines returned from the query *liberal** in both 2004 campaign speeches files (31 hits found for Bush 2004, 1 hit found for Kerry 2004) and further investigations into the source texts indicate that Bush used similar tactics as Dole to criticize his opponent's liberalism. Bush saw Kerry's liberal record as something to be repeatedly denounced, while reading the concordance line for the only hit found in Kerry's speeches file shows that Kerry tried to put the divisive labels aside and replace them by the much more encompassing label "Americans".

As one can read in the following excerpt from Bush's 2004 campaign rhetoric, Bush emulated Dole's rhetoric in his denouncing his opponent's attempt to appear conservative. Also worth noting are the social conservative issues gravitating around Bush's attacks against Kerry's liberalism:

And now, just last weekend, he even tried to claim he was the candidate with conservative values. . . . Believe it or not, that's what he said. It's hard to square that statement with his previous statement when he said, "I'm a **liberal** and proud of it." On issue after issue, from funding our troops who are on the battlefield, to involving parents in important decisions of their minor daughters, to supporting faith-based and community organizations that are helping those in need, the Senator is out of step with the mainstream values that are so important to our country.

(Bush, July 9, 2004. Remarks in York,
Pennsylvania [emphasis mine])

In addition to containing a much lower relative frequency for the query *liberal\** (rel. freq. 0.05), McCain's 2008 rhetoric appears more conciliatory in its critique against liberalism. Interestingly, McCain actually saluted some politicians for their liberal principles on the grounds that they were nonetheless willing to collaborate with people holding different political views:

Those were the attributes that distinguished Mo Udall in his public and his personal life. He was a man of great accomplishment in a tough business. But he remained throughout his life and career, a man of uncommon decency, with firm **liberal** principles but intent on finding common ground with people of different political views in order to serve his country better.

(McCain, April 5, 2008. Remarks in Prescott,
Arizona [emphasis mine])

The words uttered by McCain above seem to be in tune with his record of collaboration with people on both sides of the political spectrum and his "Maverick" figure that he pushed forward during the 2008 campaign. Yet as the successor of Bush in 2004 and Dole in 1996, McCain too considered it necessary to denounce liberalism as a negative force behind Obama's voting record and political agenda (e.g. lines 5, 6, and 7, Figure 3.13). Likewise, McCain equated liberalism with softness on foreign policy issues (e.g. lines 8, 9, 11, 12, 13 and 14, Figure 3.13).

On the other side of the spectrum, Obama tried to explain how the stakes awaiting America had little to do with the conservative/liberal divide but were important to all Americans (see Figure 3.14).

All in all, our findings undoubtedly illuminate Nunberg's (2006) and Jouet's (2017) observations on the conservative/liberal divide. In her top-down content analysis of six specific terms in the Campaign Mapping Project database, one of which was the term *liberal*, Jarvis (2005) provides some

Concord

File   Edit   View   Compute   Settings   Windows   Help

| N | Concordance | File |
|---|---|---|
| 1 | he remained throughout his life and career, a man of uncommon decency, with firm liberal principles but intent on finding common ground with people of different political | McCain_GOP_2008.txt |
| 2 | , in turn, the Asia-Pacific region and the world. But until China moves toward political liberalization, our relationship will be based on periodically shared interests rather | McCain_GOP_2008.txt |
| 3 | of learning, universities conceived to strengthen and nurture the ideals of Western liberal political thought, and young men and women who volunteered to risk their | McCain_GOP_2008.txt |
| 4 | nothing else could." It served us well, too. Barry and Mo, a proud conservative and a liberal reformer, went to Washington to fight for what they believed was right for this | McCain_GOP_2008.txt |
| 5 | Do you want to keep it and invest it in your future, or have it taken by the most liberal person to ever run for the Presidency and the Democratic leaders who have | McCain_GOP_2008.txt |
| 6 | , who came to the Senate a few years ago and already earned the title of its most liberal member - this is the man who now presents himself as a tax cutter and | McCain_GOP_2008.txt |
| 7 | for answers. In just a few years in office, Senator Obama has accumulated the most liberal voting record in the Senate. But the old, tired, big government policies he | McCain_GOP_2008.txt |
| 8 | would our lives be had he not won election in 1980 and 1984? Does anyone believe a liberal Democratic President would have called the Soviet Union an "evil empire" or | McCain_GOP_2008.txt |
| 9 | editorial boards wrote about him. He did what he thought was right. He criticized the liberal Democrats' foreign policy of weakness and vacillation. He called for resolve | McCain_GOP_2008.txt |
| 10 | inequality poses a threat to stability and free market democracy. As we pursue liberalized trade, we must work with Latin American governments to open up real | McCain_GOP_2008.txt |
| 11 | empire" or would have stood up to the nuclear freeze movement? Can you imagine a liberal Democratic President saying communism should be left on the ash heap of | McCain_GOP_2008.txt |
| 12 | empire" or would have stood up to the nuclear freeze movement? Can you imagine a liberal Democratic President saying communism should be left on the ash heap of | McCain_GOP_2008.txt |
| 13 | would our lives be had he not won election in 1980 and 1984? Does anyone believe a liberal Democratic President would have called the Soviet Union an "evil empire" or | McCain_GOP_2008.txt |
| 14 | editorial boards wrote about him. He did what he thought was right. He criticized the liberal Democrats' foreign policy of weakness and vacillation. He called for resolve | McCain_GOP_2008.txt |

*Figure 3.13* Concordance lines (14 hits) returned from the query *liberal\** in the 2008 GOP presidential campaign speeches file

Concord

File   Edit   View   Compute   Settings   Windows   Help

| N | Concordance | File |
|---|---|---|
| 1 | trade and reform. This agenda starts with education. Whether you're conservative or liberal, Republican or Democrat, practically every economist agrees that in this | Obama_Dem_2008.txt |
| 2 | sense and a politics of pragmatism. The test of an idea must not be whether it is liberal or conservative - the test should be whether it works for the American people. | Obama_Dem_2008.txt |
| 3 | to keep America strong and competitive in the 21st century. It is not left or right – liberal or conservative – to say that we have tried it their way for eight long years | Obama_Dem_2008.txt |
| 4 | an exercise in affirmative action, that it's based solely on the desire of wide-eyed liberals to purchase racial reconciliation on the cheap. On the other end, we've heard | Obama_Dem_2008.txt |
| 5 | their child gets sick. Security and opportunity; compassion and prosperity aren't liberal values or conservative values – they're American values. Most of all, I trust the | Obama_Dem_2008.txt |

*Figure 3.14* Concordance lines (5 hits) returned from the query *liberal\** in the 2008 Democratic Party presidential campaign speeches file

quantitative measurements which—although quite rudimentary and of little use for statistical comparisons[29]—sketched out the liberal pattern that we have described at length in the present section. Combining her quantitative measurements with qualitative analyses led her to formulate a conclusion that anticipated our own findings:

> [T]he term *liberal* is drenched in ideology by the Republicans and left undefended by the Democrats. . . . While its demise in electoral politics is unquestionable (most Americans living at the dawn of the twenty-first century know that the *L* word has been stigmatized), the method of its demise shows what can happen when an organized group takes on a word and the term's natural defenders abandon it.
>
> (Jarvis 2005: 177)

As demonstrated in the present section, the GOP-led war against liberalism has been launched on several interconnected fronts, including a religiously charged culture war front, and has left visible traces in the language produced by both parties. As such, it is therefore already quite clear why the liberal pattern observed in our data can inform our quest for—and understanding of—the rhetorical God gap. But our comprehension of the liberal pattern would not be as complete without bringing into the picture another important trend that strikingly parallels the trend observed in our corpus data, and which relates to how the religious landscape in America is said to have evolved along similar conservative/liberal dividing lines. On this, Olson and Green say:

> American religion [can] no longer be understood exclusively on the basis of the traditional. . . "Protestant-Catholic-Jewish" framework. Extensive societal changes caused two dominant religious orientations to emerge in the United States by the end of World War II: (1) a theologically and politically conservative religious witness and (2) a more liberal, relativist approach to both theology and politics.
>
> (Olson and Green 2006: 455)

Interestingly, the conservative v. liberal dichotomous approach to theology AND politics that Olson and Green envision seems to tally with Jouet's aforementioned account of people increasingly endorsing a broader spectrum of conservatism (Jouet 2017: 175–178). Also interesting is the fact that the trend observed by Olson and Green was referred to by Hunter who linked it to the culture wars to which he devoted his 1991 eponymous book. He notably said:

> *At the heart of the new cultural realignment are the pragmatic alliances being formed across faith traditions.* Because of common points of vision and concern, the orthodox wings of Protestantism, Catholicism, and Judaism are forming associations with each other, as are the progressive wings of each faith community—and each set of alliances takes form in opposition to the influence the other seeks to exert in public culture. . . . [A]lthough these alliances are historically "unnatural", they have become pragmatically necessary. . . . In other words, it is increasingly difficult to speak of the Protestant position or the Catholic position or the Jewish position (or, for that matter, the Mormon or Buddhist position) vis-à-vis American public culture. Meanwhile, other kinds of differences have expanded: increasingly, the politically consequential divisions are those that separate the orthodox from the progressive *within* religious traditions. And orthodox and progressive factions of the various faiths do not speak out as isolated voices but increasingly as a common chorus. In this, the political relevance of the historical divisions between Protestant and Catholic and Christian and Jew has largely become defunct.
>
> (Hunter 1991: location 664–1418 of 5465)

Green (2007: 44) seemingly disagrees with Hunter's conclusion that historical divisions between religious traditions would have become largely irrelevant, arguing instead that this "old religion gap" that he labels "the politics of religious belonging" can still help understand much of the voting behaviour of the American people. Instead of replacing the old framework of "religious belonging" with the new framework of "religious behaving and believing", Green insists on integrating both into the study of politics and religion in America. Although we will not try to gather evidence to decide who between Hunter or Green provides the truest description, we should at least keep Green's cautionary note in mind for the analysis of the "Catholic gap" that will be conducted in Chapter 4.

No matter how insightful they might be, neither the body of scholarly research referred to in the present section of Chapter 3 nor our more precise measurements and analyses actually provide evidence that a link actually exists between (1) the liberal pattern observed in presidential campaigns and (2) the liberal/conservative framework that is said to encapsulate the latest evolution of the religious landscape in America. Clearly, the parallels between (1) and (2) are intriguing and call for future research efforts in order to verify whether both phenomena are related and if they are, to what extent. In all likelihood, both are actually part of a same—although potentially larger—phenomenon.

## Coming Next

The bilateral ecumenical usage of religion against godless Communism unearthed in Chapter 2 progressively left room for more dividing and partisan trends, as the GOP candidates redirected their religiously laden rhetoric against the Democratic Party at home. Chapter 3 has confirmed that since the late 1970s, the religious rhetoric employed in the GOP presidential campaigns has been characterized by its insistence on culture-war-related issues that are dear to those having a conservative understanding of religion. This evolution of the GOP's religious rhetoric, combined with the rather controversial nature of the culture war issues, probably explains—although partially so—why many people have fallen prey to the misconception that only the GOP would use religious language. Chapter 4 will bring evidence to the contrary.

Chapter 3 has also demonstrated that—since around the 1980s—the GOP has spared no effort in loading the term *liberal* negatively through a cumulative set of "cross-associations" (Brezina et al. 2015: 55) presenting liberalism as—*inter alia*—an anti-religion, pro-abortion, pro-gay rights, pro-big government, leftist and elitist movement disconnected with the true (read conservative) American families.

As epitomized by George W. Bush's employment of the phrase "culture of life", the GOP has produced some tailor-made messages to specific religious groups, not necessarily to serve as a religious denomination-oriented strategy, but rather to rally conservatives from all walks of life and religious backgrounds under the same conservative banner. As Chapter 4 will demonstrate, the Democratic Party shows a higher tendency to call religious denominations by their specific name, as well as a desire to galvanize voters around a more communitarian understanding of religion. Chapter 4 will also report an unexpected usage of biblical language that is quite unique to the Democratic Party and which further disproves the simplistic notion that only the Republicans would use religious language.

# Notes

1. Bush, August 3, 2004. "The Compassionate Conservative Agenda" speech, Dallas, Texas.
2. 19 hits for *stem cell\**, and 3 for the hyphenated query *stem-cell\**.
3. The 2008 Obama file returns one concordance line that relates to the stem cell research issue, and which reads: "We need to invest in biomedical research and stem cell research, so that we're at the leading edge [. . .]". (Obama, June 16, 2008. Remarks at Kettering University in Flint, Michigan).
4. Available on www.nytimes.com/2006/07/19/washington/text-stem.html (Last consulted: January 2, 2018)
5. The query *stem cell\*/embryo\** in the 1900–2008 Democratic Party Conventions returns 8 hits:

    *stem cell\**: 1 hit in the 2000 Democratic Party Convention, 2 hits in the 2004 Democratic Party Convention, and 3 hits in the 2008 Democratic Party Convention. *embryo\**: 1 hit in the 2004 Democratic Party Convention, and 1 hit in the 2008 Democratic Party Convention.

6. The Campaign Ads Corpus returned no hit for this multi word query. No hit was found for the British spelling *foetal* and *foetus\**.
7. www.nytimes.com/1992/06/24/us/bush-vetoes-bill-to-lift-ban-on-money-for-fetal-research.html (Last consulted: January 3, 2018)
8. www.focusonthefamily.com/ (Last consulted: January 3, 2018).
9. Table 3.5 contains both the relative frequency values and the number of hits (i.e. raw frequencies) found in the national party platforms. As suggested at the end of Chapter 1 (see Section 1.2.2.), a "per document" frequency value can be quite informative in its own right, and returning such information is relatively easy with the National Party Platforms corpus, hence the fact that both frequencies are provided in Table 3.5.
10. President Carter used the phrase "family values" on three different occasions: in September 28, 1977 (Remarks on Signing Proclamation 4527); in October 20, 1978 (National Family Week, Proclamation 4606); and in October 15, 1979 (Remarks at the Annual Convention of the National Conference of Catholic Charities).
11. However, some have been questioning the extent to which the GOP remains the party of family values for quite some time (see for example Martin's 2012 article, "So long the party of family values" https://edition.cnn.com/2012/01/20/opinion/martin-gop-family-values/index.html Last consulted: October 22, 2018). Recent commentators are envisioning a major shift caused by President Trump's actions against migrant families. This still hypothetical move away from the traditional family values is encapsulated in Wagner's 2018 article, "The Republican Party Moves From Family Values to White Nationalism"

(www.theatlantic.com/politics/archive/2018/06/the-gop-has-chosen-white-nationalism-over-family-values/563429/ Last consulted: October 22, 2018).

12. For more on issue ownership research, see for example Damore 2004, 2005; Doherty 2008; Kaufmann 2004.

13. *judge* was also found salient in the 1968 Democratic Party file (Humphrey 1968). However, it is not reported in Table 3.7 because candidate Humphrey mostly used *judge* as a verb and without links to the culture war issues and the appointment of judges.

14. Default settings L5 R5 search span; min. frequency of collocate: 5; stop at sentence break; sorting: raw frequency values.

15. Obtained by adding up the frequency of each queried node.

16. Other similar examples are to be found in Carter's November 1, 1980 "Remarks at a Rally with Area Residents", or else in his October 20, 1980 "speech delivered at the Meeting with the Congregation of the Concord Baptist Church and State and Local Officials".

17. 27 lines for Mondale 1984; 2 for Clinton 1992; 1 for Obama 2008.

18. More detail provided upon request.

19. 51 hits for *liberal*, 8 hits for *liberals*, 1 hit for *liberalized*.

20. Retrieved from http://corpora.lancs.ac.uk/lancsbox/help.php (Last consulted: February 21, 2018).

21. The collocate *five-justice* refers to the five (out of a total of nine) U.S. Supreme Court Judges—also called "Justices"—who are needed for a ruling to be issued by the Supreme Court. In the case of Figure 3.10, the collocate *five-justice* was produced by GOP candidate Cruz (Houston debate, December 2, 2016) who expressed his fears of seeing a majority of liberal activist judges taking over the Supreme Court. He said: "We are one liberal away from a five-justice radical leftist majority that would undermine our religious liberty; that would undermine the right to life; and that would fundamentally erase the Second Amendment right to keep and bear arms from the Constitution". Quite obviously, Cruz's rhetoric connects to the issue of judicial activism we talked about in Section 3.3. of the present book.

22. For readability's sake—and similarly to Figure 3.10—several collocates of the node *conservative** have been filtered out of the graph shown in Figure 3.11, to wit: /darling|groans|ninety-two|noise] . . . and|outline|ribbed|samuel|tout|approaching|insert|loads|collected|present|purple|1950s/

23. The key keyword list contains no result for *conservative** or for *conservatism*.

24. Among the 692 hits returned from the wildcard query *liberal**, there are 502 hits (72.54%) for the word *liberal*, 61 hits (8.81%) for the word *liberalism*, 8 hits (1.15%) for the word *liberalization*, 9 hits (1.30%) for the word *liberalize*, 4 hits (0.57%) for *liberalized*, 1 hit (0.14%) for *liberalizes*, 1 hit (0.14%) for *liberalizing*, 2 hits (0.28%) for *liberally*, 102 hits (14.73%) for *liberals* and 2 (0.28%) for *liberal's*. Altogether, this means that 96.38% of the results returned from the query *liberal** concern the words *liberal/liberals/liberal's/liberalism*, which all appear quite relevant to our investigations into the liberal pattern. Such a high percentage of relevant results justifies our choice to run the wildcard query *liberal** instead of a more restrictive kind of query like *liberal/liberals*. Also, the wildcard query *liberal** has been preferred over a multiword query because the statistics it returns are easier to work with and report in graphs and tables.

25. Running the query *liberal/liberals/liberalism* in the GOP and Democratic Party campaign speeches files where these nodes have been found salient (Table 3.9) returns 354 concordance lines for the GOP and 90 for the Democratic Party.
26. The Liberal Party of New York is still in existence and is still running a website: www.liberalparty.org/ (Last consulted: February 26, 2018).
27. In his speech, Stevenson said: "There have been other remarkable changes in the political scenery. Four years ago, the Republicans rallied the country against the egghead menace. I was pictured then as the leader of the longhairs—despite all surface evidence to the contrary. President Eisenhower defined an intellectual as "a man who takes more words than necessary to tell more than he knows." Things are different today. President Eisenhower no longer ridicules intellectuals and I note with some amusement that his supporters have organized a committee devoted to the care and feeding of the egghead vote. It even includes college professors. A ranking departmental official in the Eisenhower Administration has not only read a book but has even written one. . . . We are entitled to expect good things from this blood transfusion. . . . The infiltration of the intellectuals into the Republican party may or may not change these things. But it must certainly be recognized as a minor triumph of mind over matter. . . . But one thing about this campaign is unchanged. Now, as in 1952, the Republican Presidential candidate will speak in the accents of progressivism. There will be grand new talk about his design for "rebuilding" the Grand Old Party. . . . One of the curious facts in this curious year is that the new liberal Republican party seems to have room for everybody except the liberal Republicans. . . . On the whole, it seems painfully clear that the new Republicanism is no different from the old as far as its leadership is concerned. The label has changed, but not the stuff in the package" (Stevenson, September 11, 1956. Speech at the Liberal Party Of New York Convention, acceptance of Liberal Party Nomination)
28. The highest frequencies obtained in each party from the wildcard query *liberal\** (i.e. Stevenson 1956; Dole 1996, see Figure 3.12) are significantly different ($X^2$= 32.82221, difference is significant at p < 0.001 [crit. 10.82757] Stevenson 1956: 56 hits out of 144,313 words, Dole 1996: 170 hits out of 184,373 words).
29. Indeed, Jarvis worked with raw frequencies drawn from files of different sizes. Jarvis tellingly acknowledged that "it is important to note that the Campaign Mapping Project features a larger sample of texts for 1996 than for the other years under examination" (205: 180), so that the 86 occurrences of *liberal* found in her 1996 GOP file—which is the highest raw frequency observed—cannot be easily compared with findings in her other files. However, there are indeed some conclusions that can already be drawn from these raw frequency measures, although these conclusions call for more solid evidence and better quantitative data. In spite of these limitations, we must recognize the importance of the evidence that Jarvis brought to a phenomenon that past observers had illustrated through "anecdotes" only, and this for lack of any "systematic study" (Schiffer 2000: 298).

# References

Balmer, R. 2008. *God in the White House: A History: How Faith Shaped the Presidency from John F. Kennedy to George W. Bush.* New York: HarperCollins.

Berlinerblau, J. 2008. *Thumpin' It: The Use and Abuse of the Bible in Today's Presidential Politics*. Louisville: Westminster John Knox Press, 10–11.

Brezina, V., McEnery, T. and Wattam, S. 2015. Collocations in Context: A New Perspective on Collocation Networks. *International Journal of Corpus Linguistics*, Vol. 20, No. 2, 139–173.

Clermont, B. 2009. *The Neo-Catholics: Implementing Christian Nationalism in America*. Atlanta, GA: Clarity Press, Inc.

Clymer, A. 1992. Bush Vetoes Bill to Lift Ban on Money for Fetal Research. *The New York Times*, June 24. www.nytimes.com/1992/06/24/us/bush-vetoes-bill-to-lift-ban-on-money-for-fetal-research.html Last consulted: January 3, 2018.

Damore, D. F. 2004. The Dynamics of Issue Ownership in Presidential Campaigns. *Political Research Quarterly*, Vol. 57, No. 3 (September), 391–397.

Damore, D. F. 2005. Issue Convergence in Presidential Campaigns. *Political Behavior*, Vol. 27, No. 1 (March), 71–97.

Doherty, D. 2008. Presidential Rhetoric, Candidate Evaluations, and Party Identification: Can Parties "Own" Values? *Political Research Quarterly*, Vol. 61, No. 3 (September), 419–433.

Domke, D. and Coe, K. 2008. *The God Strategy: How Religion Became a Political Weapon in America*. New York: Oxford University Press.

Dowland, S. 2009. "Family Values" and the Formation of a Christian Right Agenda. *Church History*, Vol. 78, No. 3 (September), 606–631.

Edsall, T. B. 2006. *Building Red America: The New Conservative Coalition and the Drive for Permanent Power*. New York: Basic Books.

Edwards, G. C. III. 2003. *On Deaf Ears: The Limits of the Bully Pulpit*. New Haven: Yale University Press, 74–75.

Gentile, E. 2008. *God's Democracy: American Religion After September 11*, trans. Pudney, J. and Jaus, S. D. Wesport, CT: Praeger Publishers.

Green, J. C. 2007. *The Faith Factor: How Religion Influences American Elections*. Westport, CT: Praeger Publishers.

Green, J. C., Rozell, M. J. and Wilcox, C. (eds.). 2006. *The Values Campaign? The Christian Right and the 2004 Elections*. Washington, DC: Georgetown University Press.

Hoey, M. 2005. *Lexical Priming: A new theory of words and language*. Abingdon, Oxon: Routledge.

Hunter, J. D. 1991. *Culture Wars: The Struggle to Define America*. New York: Basic Books. Kindle eBook.

Jarvis, S. E. 2005. *The Talk of the Party: Political Labels, Symbolic Capital, and American Life*. Lanham, MD: Rowman & Littlefield Publishers, Inc.

Jouet, M. 2017. *Exceptional America: What Divides Americans from the World and from Each Other*. Oakland, CA: University of California Press.

Kaufmann, K. M. 2004. Disaggregating and Reexamining Issue Ownership and Voter Choice. *Polity*, Vol. 36, No. 2 (January), 283–299.

Monson, J. Q. and Oliphant, J. B. 2007. Microtargeting and the Instrumental Mobilization of Religious Conservatives. In Campbell, D. E. (ed.). *A Matter of Faith: Religion in the 2004 Presidential Election*. Washington, DC: Brookings Institution Press, 95–141.

Norrander, B. and Norrander, J. 2007. Stem Cell Research. In Campbell, D. E. (ed.). *A Matter of Faith: Religion in the 2004 Presidential Election*. Washington, DC: Brookings Institution Press, 142–159.

Nunberg, G. 2006. *Talking Right: How Conservatives Turned Liberalism into a Tax-Raising, Latte-Drinking, Sushi-Eating, Volvo-Driving, New York Times-Reading, Body-Piercing, Hollywood-Loving, Left-Wing Freak Show*. New York: PublicAffairs.

Olson, L. R. and Green, J. C. 2006. The Religion Gap. *PS: Political Science and Politics*, Vol. 39, No. 3 (July), 455–459.

Petrocik, J. R., Benoit, W. L. and Hansen, G. J. 2003/2004. Issue Ownership and Presidential Campaigning, 1952–2000. *Political Science Quarterly*, Vol. 118, No. 4 (Winter), 599–626.

Prothero, S. 2007. *Religious Literacy: What Every American Needs to Know—And Doesn't*. New York: HarperOne.

Schiffer, A. J. 2000. I'm not that Liberal: Explaining Conservative Democratic Identification. *Political Behavior*, Vol. 22, No. 4 (December), 293–310.

Singh, R. 2003. *Contemporary American Politics and Society: Issues and Controversies*. London: Sage Publications Ltd.

Sullivan, A. 2008. *The Party Faithful: How and Why Democrats are Closing the God Gap*. New York: Scribner.

Vincent, A. 2014. *A Corpus Linguistics Approach to the Rhetorical God Gap in U.S. Presidential Campaigns*. Unpublished PhD thesis, Louvain-la-Neuve: Centre for English Corpus Linguistics, Université Catholique de Louvain.

Wilcox, C., Merolla, L. M. and Beer, D. 2006. Saving Marriage by Banning Marriage: The Christian Right Finds a New Issue in 2004. In Green, J. C., Rozell, M. J. and Wilcox, C. (eds.). *The Values Campaign? The Christian Right and the 2004 Elections*. Washington, DC: Georgetown University Press, 56–75.

Wilcox, C. and Robinson, C. 2007. Prayers, Parties, and Preachers: The Evolving Nature of Political and Religious Mobilization. In Wilson, J. M. (ed.). *From Pews to Polling Places: Faith and Politics in the American Religious Mosaic*. Washington, DC: Georgetown University Press. Kindle eBook. Location 86–430 of 3980.

# 4 The Religious Rhetoric of the Democratic Party

## Religious Denominations, Communities of Brothers and Sisters and Biblically Inspired Language

In Chapter 3, we saw that a large share of the religious rhetoric character-istically produced by the GOP is directly connected to culture war issues and the conservative/liberal divide. Also in Chapter 3, we have shown that—although it has not beaten a total retreat—the Democratic Party has either lost or else abandoned some considerable ground on the culture-war-related rhetorical front and in the defence of the term *liberal*. It seems reasonable to posit that the American culture wars and the conservative/ liberal divide have been highly controversial and have therefore grabbed most of the attention, probably at the expense of other issues. It is likely that in the process, many people have paid minimal or no attention to other forms of religious rhetoric if employed to articulate worldviews and opinions that are not part of the conservative agenda. This may in turn explain—although only partially so—why the Democratic Party's reli-gious rhetoric has been thought to be marginal, less visible, rare or even purely non-existent. As we have already shown and will further demon-strate in the present chapter, the Democratic Party has not avoided reli-gious rhetoric. Quite on the contrary, our corpus linguistic analyses reveal that it has actually produced its very specific rhetorical signature in gen-eral campaign speeches, be it by calling religious denominations by their name (Section 4.1), by articulating their vision of welfare and mutual aid with religiously laden justifications that seem rooted in a communitarian understanding of religion (Section 4.2), or else by referring to the Bible and actually quoting verbatim from it (Section 4.3). The remainder of Chapter 4 discusses each finding in turn.

## 4.1. Calling Religious Groups by Their Name: Focus on the Catholic Pattern

As argued in Chapter 3, there are some striking parallels between (1) the GOP's insistence—in its campaign rhetoric—on the conservative/liberal divide and (2) the conservative/liberal framework that scholars use to explain the new contours of the religious landscape in America (see Chapter 3, Section 4). The pattern reported in Table 4.1 seems to suggest that the Democratic Party has taken a different route from the one taken by the GOP and has insisted on terms that echo the old framework of religious belonging.

When looking at the results from a distance, the overall graphical sense one gets is that of a Democratic-Party-leaning tendency to call religious denominations by their specific name.

A cursory key keyword analysis run at a very early stage of this research project returned *catholic* as a salient keyword in more than half[1] the 1952–1996 Democratic Party campaign speeches files when tested against a reference wordlist computed from the 1952–1996 GOP campaign speeches files. No such recurring saliency was identified for the other religious groups reported in Table 4.1. When directly tested against the GOP files, *catholic* thus appears more representative of the Democratic Party's rhetoric than the other keywords in Table 4.1. In what follows, we will therefore lay the focus on *catholic* and briefly analyze how it behaves in the 1952–2008 Democratic Party campaign rhetoric. As to the other elements of Table 4.1, they will be left untouched in the present book but surely call for future research attention.

*Table 4.1* Religious Denominations Pattern (Key keyword analysis, PCS corpus, rel. freq. per 1,000 words)

| Republican Party | Year | Democratic Party |
|---|---|---|
| – | 1952 | – |
| – | 1956 | – |
| quaker (0.01) | 1960 | – |
| no 1964 GOP file | 1964 | – |
| quaker (0.01) | 1968 | – |
| – | 1972 | catholic (0.14), methodist (0.03) |
| – | 1976 | baptist (0.08) |
| – | 1980 | baptist (0.04) |
| – | 1984 | baptists (0.05), methodist (0.05), methodists (0.14), presbyterians (0.14), lutherans (0.14) |
| jewish (0.24) | 1988 | – |
| – | 1992 | catholic (0.10), baptist (0.04), baptists (0.02) |
| buddhist (0.08) | 1996 | – |
| – | 2004 | muslim (0.11) |
| islamic (0.37) | 2008 | – |

Right from the start, it seems important to make one point perfectly clear: the term *catholic* must not be seen as the only way to refer to that specific religious group. Although we will provide evidence that it can be viewed as specific to the Democratic Party campaign rhetoric—or at least to the rhetoric of several among its presidential candidates—we must not forget that other candidates did refer or even appeal to Catholics through various—and sometimes less direct—means (see for example Bush's usage of *culture of life* discussed in Chapter 3; also see Gentile 2008: 61; Edsall 2006: 91 quoted in Clermont 2009: 149–150).

Figure 4.1 plots the relative frequencies returned from the wildcard query *catholic\**[2] in the 1952–2008 PCS corpus. What graphically transpires from Figure 4.1 is an uninterrupted although fluctuating pattern where the Democratic candidates use *catholic\** more frequently than their GOP counterparts.

Evaluating the extent to which *catholic\** can be considered as a specific feature of a certain Democratic Party genre is probably a matter of perspective, and the picture one gets from the results changes according to how one approaches them. On aggregate, the 1952–2008 Democratic Party campaign rhetoric is marked by a significantly higher relative frequency than the 1952–2008 GOP campaign rhetoric ($X^2$= 64.36587, difference is significant at p <0.001). Also, every single Democratic Party candidate scored a higher relative frequency than his GOP opponent (Figure 4.1). These are both quantitative facts that can serve to describe the "Catholic gap" observed in presidential campaign rhetoric. Yet cutting reality into smaller pieces and comparing candidates running during a same campaign year

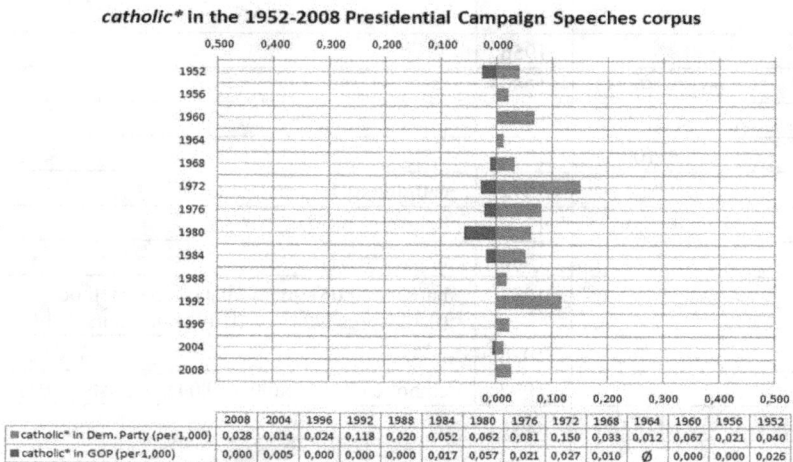

*catholic\** in the 1952-2008 Presidential Campaign Speeches corpus

| | 2008 | 2004 | 1996 | 1992 | 1988 | 1984 | 1980 | 1976 | 1972 | 1968 | 1964 | 1960 | 1956 | 1952 |
|---|---|---|---|---|---|---|---|---|---|---|---|---|---|---|
| catholic* in Dem. Party (per 1,000) | 0,028 | 0,014 | 0,024 | 0,118 | 0,020 | 0,052 | 0,062 | 0,081 | 0,150 | 0,033 | 0,012 | 0,067 | 0,021 | 0,040 |
| catholic* in GOP (per 1,000) | 0,000 | 0,005 | 0,000 | 0,000 | 0,000 | 0,017 | 0,057 | 0,021 | 0,027 | 0,010 | Ø | 0,000 | 0,000 | 0,026 |

*Figure 4.1 catholic\** in the 1952–2008 PCS corpus (rel. freq. per 1,000 words)

against each other shows that the differences separating them is statistically significant on four occasions only: in 1960 ($X^2$= 25.10785, difference is significant at p < 0.001), 1972 ($X^2$ = 8.68604, difference is significant at p <0.01), 1992 ($X^2$ = 29.78264, difference is significant at p <0.001) and 2008 ($X^2$ = 6.15315, difference is significant at p <0.05).[3]

Two GOP-specific features appearing in Figure 4.1 deserve some attention. First, while the Democratic Party used *catholic\** uninterruptedly despite fluctuating frequencies, the *catholic\** pattern on the GOP side is made of three unequal waves. Each wave is followed by several campaigns where *catholic\** is nowhere to be found. The transient nature of these waves is intriguing and poses the question—unanswered in this book—of why several GOP candidates felt the urge to use *catholic\** while others refrained from using it entirely.

Also of interest in Figure 4.1 is the relative frequency peak located on the 1980 Reagan campaign. There is a significant difference ($X^2$ = 14.59801, difference is significant at p < 0.01) between Reagan 1980 (5 hits, 0.056 per 1,000 words) and the aggregate relative frequency score obtained by the prior and following GOP campaigns (22 hits, 0.008 per 1,000 words). The literature is replete with examples where Reagan is described as a key figure of a religious-cum-conservative revolution and as the most talented strategist of what Domke and Coe (2008) label the "God Strategy". Whether the higher frequency observed for *catholic\** in Reagan's rhetoric results from the conservative revolution context in general—and from Reagan's very own "God Strategy" in particular—will not be investigated here. Some authors however provide interesting clues and comments as to the relationship Reagan established with Catholics. Clermont for example notes:

> Reagan used his friendship with Pope John Paul II to solidify Catholic support for the Republican Party. In addition to his several meetings with the pope, Reagan spoke before the Knights of Malta, the Knights of Columbus, the Heritage Foundation of Easter Europeans, Catholic universities and other organizations.
>
> (Clermont 2009: 96)

In a similar fashion, Smith says:

> The Reagan administration also took many steps to try to establish good rapport with Catholics, who had become a major force in American politics. . . . Reagan spoke to many Catholic groups, typically discussing abortion, school prayer, tuition tax credits, and volunteerism and often quoting Pope John Paul II and Catholic theologians and authors. Catholics played many important roles in the Reagan White

House. . . . Three Catholic lay organizations, most of whose members were blue-collar Reagan Democrats, especially supported his social policies: the Knights of Columbus, the Catholic Daughters of America, and the Catholic Golden Age.

(Smith 2006: 340–341)

Clermont and Smith's accounts notwithstanding, the relative frequencies of *catholic\** in Reagan's campaign speeches sometimes pale in comparison to those found in several Democratic Party files. In total, his 1980–1984 GOP speeches contain 9 *catholic\** hits only, which may appear as a rather low score for someone who is described as so willing to bond with Catholics. In turn, it seems fair to ask why Reagan did not use more direct references to Catholicism if he had been so willing to connect with them. Smith (2006) argues that direct appeals to Catholics were deemed politically risky by Reagan and his staff. He then explains that the GOP chose—among other electoral manoeuvres—to insist on moral and culture-war issues and to exploit the conservative/liberal divide rather than appeal directly to specific religious traditions. In other words, the Catholics that the GOP decided to court were not so much courted through their Catholicism as through their conservatism. This further supports the findings reported in Chapter 3.

If we can claim from our statistical measures in the PCS corpus that *catholic\** can be viewed as one ingredient of the Democratic Party religious rhetoric arsenal, several questions then immediately rush to mind: Does *catholic\** indicate that the Democratic Party tries to appeal to this particular religious constituency? Is this a form of "God Strategy" (see Domke and Coe 2008) and if it is, has it been successful?[4] Is there any special relationship between Catholics and the Democratic Party? Other questions could be: To what extent have the Democratic Party candidates understood the conservative/liberal divide and the growing obsolescence of the traditional divide between religious denominations? Why have they insisted on *catholic\** in spite of this new divide? How can we reconcile such insistence in their rhetoric with the fact that they have progressively lost support from Catholics nonetheless? Answering all these questions clearly falls beyond the scope of the present book and requires much more research from disciplines outside of the corpus linguistics realm alone. The "Catholic vote" must be approached as a complex phenomenon driven by forces that are multiple and not easy to grasp (Steinfel 2007: 357–358; for more on the Catholic vote and the Democratic Party, see Clermont 2009; Gray et al. 2006; Steinfel 2007; Streb and Frederick 2008; Wilson 2007).

In addition to quantitative differences across time and party lines, we can also observe fluctuation between campaigns run by the same candidate. This is notably the case with Clinton, whose usage of *catholic\** decreased quite significantly between 1992 and 1996[5] (Figure 4.1). Such fluctuation raises several interesting questions: Provided *catholic\** can be viewed as one ingredient of the Democratic rhetorical package, could one actually claim that Clinton sounded less Democratic in 1996 than in 1992? Or is this difference to be attributed to something else, like the fact that Clinton was an incumbent president running for re-election in 1996 and therefore had to adopt a more presidential-sounding register? What kind of influence might contextual factors like the religiously charged 1992–1995 Bosnian War have had on the religious references used by Clinton? Once again, these questions will be left unanswered here.

The fluctuating nature of the *catholic\** pattern does not concern relative frequencies only. If the relative frequencies obtained from the query *catholic\** in the 1952–2008 Presidential Campaign Speeches corpus (Figure 4.1) are compared with the dispersion values[6] obtained from the same query (Figure 4.2), we can see that the candidates who used *catholic\** the most in terms of relative frequency are not necessarily those who peppered their rhetoric with *catholic\** in an evenly spread manner.

The dispersion values presented in Figure 4.2 may lead to other exciting questions. Among them, we can think of the extent to which low dispersion values could indicate a desire to narrowcast and send specific religious signals to specific audiences. These low dispersion values also pose the question of whether a candidate refrained from using a specific word too regularly, yet sometimes had to. This second explanation most probably applies to the dispersion and relative frequency values observed for 1960

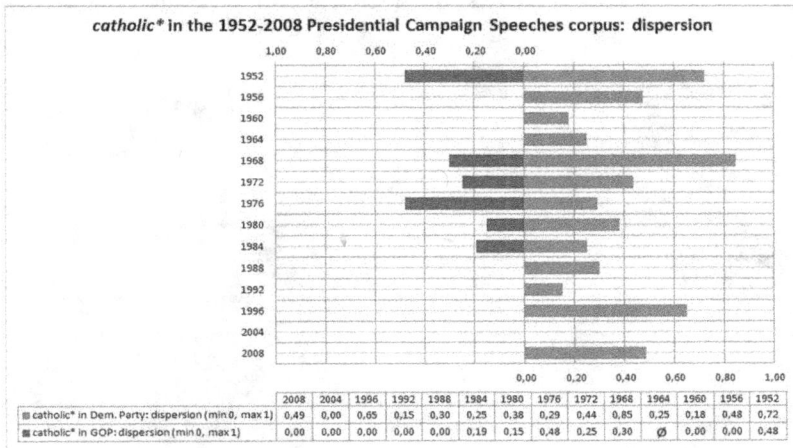

catholic* in the 1952-2008 Presidential Campaign Speeches corpus: dispersion

| | 2008 | 2004 | 1996 | 1992 | 1988 | 1984 | 1980 | 1976 | 1972 | 1968 | 1964 | 1960 | 1956 | 1952 |
|---|---|---|---|---|---|---|---|---|---|---|---|---|---|---|
| catholic* in Dem. Party: dispersion (min 0, max 1) | 0,49 | 0,00 | 0,65 | 0,15 | 0,30 | 0,25 | 0,38 | 0,29 | 0,44 | 0,85 | 0,25 | 0,18 | 0,48 | 0,72 |
| catholic* in GOP: dispersion (min 0, max 1) | 0,00 | 0,00 | 0,00 | 0,00 | 0,00 | 0,19 | 0,15 | 0,48 | 0,25 | 0,30 | ∅ | 0,00 | 0,00 | 0,48 |

*Figure 4.2* Dispersion values returned from the query *catholic\** in the 1952–2008 PCS corpus

Catholic candidate Kennedy, who had to take a test about his Catholicism and, at some point, had to address it while trying as much as he could to avoid referring to his Catholicism given how wary many voters were about it, hence the low dispersion value.

Some more qualitative analyses of the term *catholic* have led to other interesting findings. One of them—reported below—relates to the differences separating the religious right from the religious left, and to the split opposing an individualistic way of being religious to a more communitarian understanding of religion and mutual aid. This discovery was made while analyzing how Clinton used *catholic\** in his campaign speeches in general (27 hits in total), and in his 11 September 1992 Notre Dame speech more specifically (21 hits out of 27). As apparent in Figure 4.3 (concordance lines 17 to 21), Clinton praised the Catholics for their social interventions in the American society and claimed to be drawn to—and even share—this social penchant. This openly expressed support for the Catholics and their actions is something that context would not easily permit in prior times—notably during Kennedy's campaign—when suspicion towards the Catholics and the Vatican was still rampant. In this, Clinton's use of the word *catholic* constitutes a departure from the way *catholic* was used during the candidacy of Kennedy.

One specific feature of Clinton's campaign rhetoric is the link that he establishes between the word *social* and the word *catholic*. A strong relationship exists between the words *catholic* and *social* in Clinton's 1992 campaign speeches. Indeed, computing the collocation relationship strength (MI-score) between the node *social* and the collocate *catholic* (5 occurrences for this collocation) in Clinton's 1992 campaign rhetoric shows that the collocation is statistically strong (MI-score: 11.242, significant if $\geq 3$).

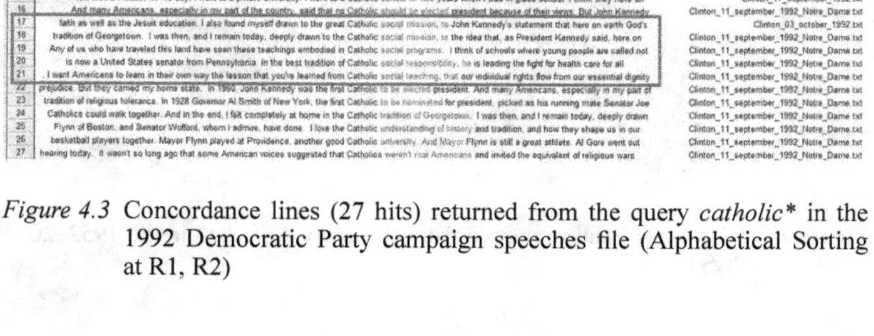

*Figure 4.3* Concordance lines (27 hits) returned from the query *catholic\** in the 1992 Democratic Party campaign speeches file (Alphabetical Sorting at R1, R2)

Likewise, the certainty of the relationship, though less impressive, is still found significant by the T-score test[7] (2.235, significant if ≥2). Each of the 5 instances of this collocation finds *catholic* as a direct left collocate of the node *social*, as reported in Figure 4.3. From this, we get a sense that Clinton often placed social action not very far from religious aspirations. It is then interesting to read Sullivan's account:

> The idea that religion could be a force for good in individuals' lives—and perhaps even provide a salve for some social ills—was not new to Clinton. But he was becoming keenly aware that this understanding that he had always taken for fact might be a radical thought to many within his party and perhaps even to members of his own staff. "Sometimes," he mused aloud to the audience, "I think the environment in which we operate is entirely too secular."
>
> (Sullivan 2008: 83)

From the very start of the present book, we have highlighted several biases that are still present in the mainstream understanding of the God gap. To these shortcomings, we can add Mockabee et al.'s critique levelled at the traditional measures of religiosity in America, which in their view favour a conservative and individualistic way of religion and ignore the existence—proved real by Mockabee et al's findings—of a communitarian religiosity leaning towards liberalism and large-scale solidarity (Mockabee et al. 2009). Interestingly enough, Mockabee et al. put historic Catholicism into this second category. Citing other scholars, they explain:

> In a series of studies of Catholic datasets, Leege and associates (1988, 1991) have shown that individualistic religious norms that approximate American evangelical practice are associated with political conservatism and personal responsibility for ameliorating social ills, while communitarian religious norms like those of historic Catholicism are associated with political liberalism and collective responsibility for overcoming social ills.
>
> (Mockabee et al. 2009: 4)

Several pieces of the religious-cum-political jigsaw seem to fall into place, as the associations between its driving forces become more distinguishable. This is notably the case with the liberal/conservative divide whose links with the communitarian/individualistic divide are showing through in the quotation above.

If Mockabee et al. are to be trusted, serving others, social responsibility and collective action (2009: 2–5) are three ingredients that best describe the communitarian way of religion and those who altogether form what

Mockabee et al. label the religious left. Whether Clinton's views on solidarity and his insistence on communitarian concerns and on the Catholic social mission can be held as a strategic appeal to the liberal-leaning religious left cannot be proved by corpus linguistic evidence. Nor can we know whether the religious left is actually drawn to and influenced by such appeals. These will therefore remain pending questions. The only thing that can be said so far is that there seems to be some common ground between Clinton's rhetoric and the core concerns of the religious left.

Fortunately, some scholars provide complementary insights into the God gap, the political dimensions of Catholicism and the individualistic/communitarian divide. This is the case with Sullivan (2008), who denounces the heavy responsibility that the liberal Democrats share for the inception of a God gap that they are traditionally seen as the victims—not the initiators—of. Sullivan contends that the Democrats progressively lost touch with religious people. She explains how the Democrats and liberals "chose to beat a retreat in the competition for religious voters and the discussion of morality, effectively ceding the ground to conservatives" (Sullivan 2008: 6–7). Sullivan forcefully argues that "[t]he emergence of the God gap represents a failure of the left as much as it does an achievement of the right" (Ibid.). Later in her book, Sullivan confirms a certain penchant for communitarianism on the part of the Democratic Party. However, she explains that the Democrats' inclination towards communitarianism was progressively restricted to economic considerations and replaced in the social sphere by a much more individualistic—and uncompromising—agenda. She says:

> Over the previous two decades, liberals had taken extremely worthy positions—equal rights and opportunities for women (including reproductive freedom), civil rights for racial minorities, acceptance of homosexuality, and a willingness to acknowledge that the model of a nuclear family no longer described many American households—and raised them to the level of doctrinal fetishes. Support of equal rights for women quickly morphed into a pro-choice litmus test for presidential nominees. Celebration of civil rights for minorities somehow resulted in opposition to any attempts at reforming the welfare system. Instead of developing a political philosophy that balanced individual rights against the common good, liberal Democrats had replaced communitarianism with individualism, at least in the social sphere. They believed that people had economic responsibilities to each other that required them to support a minimum wage, welfare programs, and efforts to hold corporations accountable. But liberals drew the line at acknowledging the effect personal actions had on the community. Choices, they insisted, were private and sacrosanct.
>
> (Sullivan 2008: 86–87)

Sullivan's account suggests that—among the religious voters that they progressively lost—the Democrats probably alienated many of those who belonged to the religious left and experienced religion in a more communitarian way.

As regards the Catholics more specifically, and the way the Democratic Party slowly lost touch with them, Sullivan recounts:

> In 1972, McGovern and his allies hadn't known what to say to Catholic voters. By 1988, Democrats had just stopped talking to them. Republicans could not have been more thrilled. . . . Any reasonably populist Democrat would have posed a serious challenge to the vice president. But in choosing the wooden, secular, technocratic Dukakis, Democrats had found that rare politician who actually made Bush seem in touch with average Americans.
>
> (Sullivan 2008: 89)[8]

Commenting on Clinton's position towards the Catholics, Sullivan then explains how—within such a context—Clinton "sought out the Catholic audiences Dukakis had avoided" (Sullivan 2008: 90) and tried to reanimate the social communitarianism that the liberals had slowly abandoned (Sullivan 2008: 92–93). If Sullivan is right, it thus seems reasonable to posit that Clinton tried to reconnect with the religious left. His insisting on the Catholic social agenda (see supra, *social/catholic* collocation) must probably be interpreted as part of the same effort to reconnect with those cultivating a more communitarian understanding of religion. The following low-key interview—given by Clinton to a Catholic reporter while on the campaign trail—is quite enlightening in this respect:

> [Clinton] was musing aloud about the dual influence of his Baptist heritage and Catholic schooling. "From my Southern Baptist heritage . . . I have a deep belief that the First Amendment separation between church and state is what guarantees the religious freedom of all people. . . . " Catholics, as Clinton knew, have a much more complicated approach to the church/state relationship. So, warming to the topic, he shrewdly pivoted to draw a distinction that favored Catholics. The experience of studying at Georgetown . . . taught him "that we are morally obliged to try to live out our religious convictions in the world, that our obligation to social mission is connected to religious life . . . That I got out of my Catholic training more than from the Baptist Church, which is much more rooted in the notion that salvation is a matter of personal relationship between an individual and God and carries with it no necessary burden to go out into the world and do things".
>
> (Sullivan 2008: 94)

From this interview, one gets a sense that the difference between the individualistic and the communitarian ways of being religious was something that Clinton understood and wanted to exploit. The way he talked about this polarity in the interview indicates that he actually tried to appeal to and reconcile both poles, with his own persona epitomizing the feasibility of putting together what comes otherwise as antithetical ways of being religious.

Sullivan seems to imply that—because of its exceptional character when compared to the Democratic Party campaigns previously or subsequently run—Clinton's approach to religion informs us about Clinton only, and not about the Democratic Party:

> Bill Clinton would leave the White House as the most overtly religious president the country had ever seen, a man who could quote biblical passages chapter and verse. . . . The policies of the Clinton administration would have a greater impact on religious freedom and liberty than any of his predecessors' going back to James Madison. And yet for all these achievements, the president could never convince his party to take religion—and religious voters—seriously. When he left office, Clinton's approach to religion left with him.
>
> (Sullivan 2008: 84)

Sullivan undoubtedly provides interesting insights, but a healthy dose of scepticism is nonetheless required as regards her unsubstantiated claim that Clinton's overt religiosity had been unequalled. In all likelihood, other scholars have awarded other presidents the same number one position, while providing little evidence to confirm that such position is truly deserved. In case we can trust Sullivan and go with the fact that Clinton does constitute some kind of singularity in the political religious sphere, there are still qualifications to be made.

The first one is provided by Sullivan herself, who—in the last chapters of her book (2008: 153–220)—hints at the 2004 campaign aftermath as a key turning point featuring Democratic Party figures who got religion at last, broke with the blunders and unease of their predecessors and were—by all appearances—quite happy to engage in religious discussions. The "Democrats' turnabout"—as Sullivan calls it (2008: 210)—leads her to amend her book title with a telling caption that reads "How and Why Democrats Are Closing the God Gap".

The second point that seems to suggest that Clinton has not been entirely alone in his religiously informed communitarianism comes from two sets of results drawn from our PCS corpus. The first set of results comes from a keyword analysis, the description of which follows immediately below (Section 4.2.1). The second set of results comes from our main key keyword analysis and will be referred to as the "brotherhood pattern" (Section 4.2.2).

Both sets of results indicate that a concern for communitarian and social matters has been saliently and recurrently expressed in the Democratic Party campaign speeches, and sometimes with hints of a religiously tinted language. If, according to Sullivan, Clinton's own approach to religion left the White House with him, both sets of data show that not all of the language that intersects with the core concerns of the religious left and a communitarian mindset disappears in the pre- or post-Clinton era.

## 4.2. A Community of Brothers and Sisters

### 4.2.1. Keyword Analysis: 1952–2008 Democratic Party Campaign Speeches Wordlist (minus Clinton 1992–1996) versus 1952–2008 GOP Campaign Speeches Wordlist

An aggregate wordlist was computed on the basis of all the Democratic Party campaign speeches files minus those of Clinton 1992 and 1996. Removing Clinton's 1992 and 1996 campaign speeches from the present analysis is meant to help us determine whether other Democratic Party candidates shared with Clinton some of his religiously informed communitarian language. The reference wordlist used in this keyword analysis was computed directly from the 1952–2008 GOP Presidential Campaign speeches. Both wordlists were then compared, and a list of statistically salient keywords—amounting to a total of 1,331 of them—returned accordingly. The default settings were left unchanged, i.e. a p-value of 0.000001 and a minimum frequency cutoff of 3. Only the "maximum number of results" threshold was set to a higher value than the default one to integrate all the positive keywords returned by the *Keyword* program.

What we get from this keyword analysis are tentative results only. Several limitations forbid seeing them otherwise. For one, a reference corpus of campaign rhetoric constitutes a powerful filter, and it might be methodologically questionable to combine it with a p-value that is quite low and therefore functions as another powerful filter. Also, we know from the corpus descriptions made in Chapter 1 that each file varies in size. An aggregate wordlist must thus be seen with some caution, as the impact that one file can have on the overall picture may be much greater than that of the other files.

Although tentative, the results are interesting in that they together provide some evidence that the Democratic Party rhetoric has been saliently marked by two semantic categories, here labelled "social mission" and "community" (Table 4.2).

In labelling the semantic categories reported in Table 4.2 "social mission" and "community", the connections with Clinton's rhetoric and the religious left's key concerns are implied quite explicitly but cannot be taken as proven. These categories are the product of subjectivity and interpretation

*Table 4.2* "social mission" and "community": Democratic Party-specific semantic categories (keyword analysis:1952–2008 Democratic Party Campaign Speeches wordlist [minus Clinton 1992–1996] v. 1952–2008 GOP Campaign Speeches wordlist)

| *social mission* (N= log-likelihood keyness value) | | *community* (N= log-likelihood keyness value) | |
|---|---|---|---|
| *aid*: 107.38 | *social*: 87.36 | *our*: 196.04 | *together*: 283.16 |
| *cared*: 65.88 | *socialism*: 127.70 | *ourselves*: 49.51 | *unity*: 41.72 |
| *help*: 58.70 | | *us*: 84.20 | *union*: 38.92 |
| *justice*: 105.93 | *unequal*: 36.69 | *join*: 101.48 | *divide*: 67.94 |
| *discrimination*: 53.75 | *equal*: 69.93 | *community*: 29.94 | *divided*: 96.18 |
| *discriminating*: 53.42 | *equality*: 28.54 | *common*: 105.75 | *division*: 46.39 |
| | | | *divisions*: 40.32 |
| *hunger*: 46.66 | *elderly*: 80.62 | *country*: 610.54 | |
| *hungry*: 59.18 | *handicapped*: 61.29 | *nation*: 261.12 | |
| | *sick*: 75.52 | *universal*: 29.20 | |
| *homeless*: 27.46 | *poverty*: 208.58 | | |
| *slum*: 43.62 | *poor*: 30.29 | | |
| *slums*: 50.54 | *wealthiest*: 133.98 | | |
| | *wealthy*: 79.08 | | |
| *unemployed*: 52.77 | *minimum*: 374.06 | | |
| *unemployment*: 77.64 | *wage*: 305.00 | | |
| *employment*: 101.43 | | | |
| *work*: 36.91 | | | |
| *workers*: 31.63 | | | |
| *working*: 26.72 | | | |
| *workingman*: 31.73 | | | |

from concordance reading and collocation analyses. Moreover, these categories also contain keywords that—should we further analyze their semantic prosodies and the kind of message they convey—can carry a rather negative connotation. This is notably the case with a keyword like *socialism* (Table 4.2, Column 1); examination of the concordance lines revealed a repeated effort to discuss and discard accusations—allegedly from the GOP camp—of the Democrats being socialist or even communist. This implies that some keywords may be there not necessarily out of a desire to talk about them but instead because the candidates had to address the charges levelled against them via these negatively charged words.

What seems to emerge from this brief analysis is that "getting together" and "mutual aid" constitute salient issues in the Democratic Party's rhetoric, and this is so even when Clinton is out of the picture. So, if the GOP has insisted on the liberal/conservative divide and has captured the word *liberal*, it seems that the Democratic Party has held steady in its calling for mutual aid and unity.

Whether such a call has been uttered for and heard by the liberal religious left will mostly remain unevidenced here. Two scholars provide some clues that the religious left actually heard the message of mutual aid and unity specifically addressed by the Democratic Party candidates and that the insistence on communitarian and social issues can sometimes relate to the union between politics and religion. The first scholar is—once again—Sullivan, who explains that Mara Vanderslice—the religious outreach director for the 2004 Kerry campaign—"reached out to groups of Catholic nuns, traditionally a far more liberal constituency than priests. The sisters were enthusiastic campaign workers. . . . Catholic voters who were still up in the air by October got used to the shock of picking up the phone and hearing, 'This is Sister Mary Alice calling to ask you to support John Kerry for president'" (2008: 184). From this, we understand that religious groups in general—and Catholics in this specific instance—have been the focus of tailor-made messages and energized into taking an active part in garnering votes. Then, Sullivan explains how the communitarian and social concerns that seem so typical of the Catholic tradition and of the larger religious left were clearly integrated into the campaign strategy to garner votes: "The final piece of Vanderslice's strategy was a direct-mail piece that framed Kerry's policies as efforts to improve the 'common good,' a resonant phrase from Catholic social teaching" (Ibid.).

In an evocatively titled blog article "Reaching Catholics", Arkedis (2012) provides a perspective that is slightly unusual. In this specific instance, the call to mobilize Catholics around the communitarian and social concerns is uttered *from* a Catholic voter[9] and addressed *to* the 2012 Democratic Party's campaign strategists themselves. If Arkedis is no official spokesperson for the religious left or the Catholic voters, his account nonetheless suggests that on both the Religious and Political left sides, there has been a shared understanding that communitarian and social concerns can constitute clear incentives to collaborate and side with the Democratic Party. Arkedis explains:

> Catholics are up for grabs this year [i.e. 2012]. . . . The Obama campaign's message should unequivocally stand with the church and Jesus Christ's humble message of social justice, equality and inclusion. These are distinctly Catholic themes that draw sharp contrasts for Catholics who have tired of a Republican Party with less room for those who are not straight, male, white and self-sufficient. . . . A broad, upbeat theme of social justice will be enough for Obama to reach persuadable Catholics, who can interpret the message in concert with their beliefs. . . . As a moderate Democrat and a Catholic, I disagree with my party when I say that I believe life begins at

conception or that abortions should be performed only in cases of rape, incest or when a pregnancy threatens a mother's life. In another era, those beliefs might have made me a Republican target. But I'm a Democrat, in part, because of the party's deep belief in social justice: We're the ones who make equality and inclusion central to our very being; we stick up for the little guy; we don't believe everyone should fend for themselves all the time. That's what Jesus said, and that's the society President Obama wants to build.

(Arkedis 2012)

Arkedis turns even more strategic as he encourages the Obama campaign to tailor its messages according to where persuadable Catholics live:

Newly available data show the Obama campaign exactly where to target persuadable Catholics. . . . They heavily populate the Northeast, the upper Midwest, south Florida, southern Colorado and northern New Mexico, and California. In other words, there are a lot of Catholics in crucial swing states. . . . Overlaying a map of densely Catholic counties on top of a map of persuadable voters shows that the Obama re-election team has a unique chance to focus its social justice message on prized areas: heavily Catholic, moderate counties within swing states. . . . it's a must: a positive social justice message could be what tips the balance toward re-election for the president.

(Ibid.)

From Sullivan's account and Arkedis's paper, one gets a sense that—on both the religious and political left sides—there is a common understanding around the importance of the communitarian and social issues, and each side has shown some desire to insist on them to build alliances and increase collaboration.

### 4.2.2. The Brotherhood Pattern

Another set of results points in the direction of a Democratic Party-specific insistence on mutual aid and responsibility. These results were identified through our main key keyword analysis of the PCS corpus and altogether form what is called here the "brotherhood pattern". As graphically apparent in Table 4.3, this gap clearly tilts the balance towards the Democratic Party and seems to show a certain degree of durability.

Table 4.3 qualifies as a religiously laden pattern in and of itself, irrespective of the fact that many among the keywords it contains were used by the Democratic candidates to articulate communitarian and social concerns of the sorts mentioned earlier. The very notion

*Table 4.3* Brotherhood Pattern (Key keyword analysis, PCS corpus, rel. freq. per 1,000 words)

| Republican Party | Year | Democratic Party |
|---|---|---|
| – | 1952 | brotherhood (0.02) |
| brotherhood (0.10) | 1956 | – |
| – | 1960 | – |
| no 1964 GOP file | 1964 | – |
| – | 1968 | brotherhood (0.03) |
| – | 1972 | brotherhood (0.04) |
| – | 1976 | brotherhood (0.14), sisterhood (0.05) |
| – | 1980 | – |
| – | 1984 | brethren (0.07) |
| – | from 1988 to 1996 | – |
| – | 2004 | brothers (0.16) |
| – | 2008 | brother's (0.04), sister's (0.04) |

of brotherhood is indeed charged with religious significance and—according to O'Connell—is "an important Christian concept" (2012: 115). Also, the prominent place that the brotherhood concept occupies in the Bible can be easily evidenced by means of a simple keyword analysis opposing the King James Bible against a reference corpus of General English. Whether tested against the British National Corpus (BNC) or the OANC,[10] the King James Bible corpus returns *brethren*, *brother*, and *brother's* as statistically significant—and therefore Bible-specific—keywords.[11]

Another piece of evidence for the biblical rooting of the brotherhood concept and the religious taste that it can have in campaign rhetoric is to be found in Clinton's Notre Dame speech where one can read Clinton directly drawing from the Book of Genesis to articulate his views on mutual aid and responsibility:

I want an America with those convictions to have a renewed sense of community, an America that is coming together, not coming apart. . . . Echoing down the ages is the simple but powerful truth that no grace of God was ever given me for me alone. To the terrible question of Cain—Am I my **brother's** keeper?—the only possible answer for us is God's thunderous yes.

(Clinton, 1992. Notre Dame Speech [emphasis mine])

As apparent in Table 4.3, the 1992 and 1996 Clinton campaigns are not marked by the brotherhood pattern keywords. However, we clearly see in the Notre Dame speech that Clinton could occasionally tap into a religious—and even biblical—brotherhood reference to insist on communitarian and social issues.

With a few exceptions, the "brotherhood" key keywords produced by the Democratic Party and presented in Table 4.3 contribute to the very same biblically charged rhetoric of mutual aid and responsibility. Analyzing the keywords found on the Democratic Party side (Table 4.3) indicates that the Democrats would produce such terms while drawing from the Bible and from biblically inspired seminal speeches of the kind produced by civil religious figures such as Winthrop or Martin Luther King. No such biblical usage was found in the only GOP file marked by the keyword *brotherhood* (to wit, the 1956 campaign file), with the exception of one religiously laden passage where Eisenhower stated: "Freedom is rooted in the certainty that the brotherhood of all men springs from the fatherhood of God. And thus, even as each man is his brother's keeper, no man is another's master" (Eisenhower, November 1, 1956. Address in Conventional Hall, Philadelphia, Pennsylvania).

As stated above, Clinton's usage of the "Am I my brother's keeper" line is directly drawn from the Book of Genesis (4:9) and is inserted into a Notre Dame speech that is ripe with biblical references.

Interrogating the source texts for Mondale (1984 Democratic Party campaign) reveals that he uses the keyword *brethren* to address President Reagan's exploitation of the "city upon a hill" metaphor, which originates from Winthrop's 1630 Sermon "A Model of Christian Charity". The biblical tone of Winthrop's speech—which seems inspired by the Book of Romans[12]—reverberates through Mondale's rhetoric. Diving deeper into the concordance lines containing *brethren* reveals that he criticizes Reagan for focusing on the "city on a hill" part of the speech only and for being untrue to Winthrop's teachings about mutual responsibilities and communitarian concerns. In doing so, Mondale provides another example of a Democratic Party candidate attacking a conservative-style society and emphasizing communitarian and social concerns through religious language.

In Kerry's 2004 campaign rhetoric, *brothers* is rarely connected to religious rhetoric and to the insistence on the community and on mutual assistance, since Kerry mostly used *brothers* in combination with *band of* to refer to his experience as a military veteran. Yet on a few occasions, Kerry uses *brothers* to convey a religiously laden message and articulate his communitarian vision in a fashion that is quite reminiscent of Clinton's Notre Dame speech and Winthrop's sermon:

> In the Book of James we are taught: "It is not enough, my brother to say you have faith when there are no deeds . . . Faith without works is dead." For me, that means having and holding to a vision of a society of

the common good, where individual rights and freedoms are connected to our responsibility to others. It means understanding that the authentic role of leadership is to advance the liberty of each of us and the good that can come to all of us, when we work together as one united community. Catholics call this solidarity. We simply mean that as children of the same God, we share a common destiny. We express our humanity by reaching out to our fellow citizens, and indeed, to all our brothers and sisters in this country and on this earth. It means that the joys and hopes, the griefs and anxieties are not felt in isolation, they are shared by all.

> (Kerry, October 24, 2004. Remarks at the Broward Center for
> the Performing Arts, Fort Lauderdale, Florida)

Obama's more recent exploitation of this brotherhood theme turns out to be more inclusive as the term *sister's* becomes salient (see Table 4.3) in his exploitation of this otherwise quite traditional Democratic Party rhetoric:

So Dr. King had been to the mountaintop. He had seen the Promised Land. And while he knew somewhere deep in his bones that he would not get there with us, he knew that we would get there. He knew it because he had seen that Americans have "the capacity," as he said that night, "to project the 'I' into the 'thou.'" To recognize that no matter what the color of our skin, no matter what faith we practice, no matter how much money we have—no matter whether we are sanitation workers or United States Senators—we all have a stake in one another, we are our **brother's** keeper, we are our **sister's** keeper, and "either we go up together, or we go down together."

> (Obama, April 4, 2008. Remarks in Fort Wayne,
> Indiana [emphasis mine])

As for the *brother's keeper* line proper, running a query *brother's keeper* across the 27 campaign speeches files (22 hits) suggests a Democratic Party tendency in very broad terms (20 hits on the Democratic Party side), and reveals the existence of an Obama-specific feature (16 hits for Obama alone).[13]

As regards the term *brotherhood* and *sisterhood*, skimming through the concordance lines from the 1952, 1968, 1972 and 1976 Democratic Party files reveals that they appear less overtly religious than the other elements of Table 4.3, but are used to articulate a similar vision of mutual responsibility and community.

## 4.3. The Bible and the Democratic Party

Near the end of her 2016 concession speech to Donald Trump, Democratic Party candidate Hillary Clinton recited a few lines from the Bible. She said: "Scripture tells us: Let us not grow weary in doing good, for in due season we shall reap if we do not lose heart" (Clinton, H., November 9, 2016. "Concession Speech", New York). A few months earlier, her Republican opponent Donald Trump had been derided for his bad biblical reference to "Two Corinthians" (instead of "Second Corinthians") before a gathering of evangelical students at Liberty University (Trump, D., January 18, 2016. "Liberty University Speech", Lynchburg, Virginia). Both examples show that Bible-talk can cross party lines and does not guarantee nor forbid electoral success, no matter how good or bad it is judged to be. Some might be tempted to discount such observations on the grounds that the 2016 election was highly unusual and therefore not a good place to understand the rhetorical God gap. Although it seems fair to say that the 2016 campaign was unusual in many respects indeed, it would be wrong to see the presence of biblical language—good or bad—as another consequence of this unusual 2016 campaign.

The Bible in American politics is hardly a new phenomenon. In fact, it has been present since the very birth of the nation. In his 1630 seminal speech "A Model of Christian Charity" (which is best remembered as the "City Upon a Hill" speech), John Winthrop heavily drew on the Bible to call on the early settlers to repress their individual aspirations and work on social cohesion and the survival of the group. George Washington—who was in search of strong symbols and rituals to try to get the nascent American society to hold together—set a precedent that has survived to these days as he decided to emulate a British coronation and swore on the Bible while taking the very first presidential oath in American history (Church 2007: 35). The Bible was exploited by both camps during the 1860–1865 Civil War to articulate antagonistic views on slavery and God's intentions. These few examples from history show that the Bible has been present not just physically as some sort of civil religious prop but also through the very words produced to either contribute to a common goal or else to articulate antagonistic views.

Based on this simple historical observation, the presence of biblically inspired language in more recent campaign speeches should not be considered surprising. What might come as a surprise, however, is our discovery that—in the 1952–2008 general campaign speeches at least—the Bible is mostly present in the Democratic Party camp and turns out to be a characteristic feature of its presidential campaign rhetoric. As will be argued below, such discovery flies in the face of conventional wisdom and previous scholarly work alike.

The Democratic-Party-specific pattern of biblically inspired language (henceforward called "Bible pattern") presented in this last part of Chapter 4 is made of statistically significant words extracted from the PCS corpus via our main key keyword analysis. As can be observed in Table 4.4,[14] there has been—in the Democratic Party camp—a fluctuating yet enduring tendency

*Table 4.4* Bible Pattern (Key keyword analysis, PCS corpus, rel. freq. per 1,000 words)

| Republican Party | Year | Democratic Party |
|---|---|---|
| – | 1952 | commandments (0.02) |
| – | 1956 | – |
| – | 1960 | bible (0.05), scriptural (0.01), trumpet (0.03) |
| no 1964 GOP file | 1964 | cheek (0.04), isaiah (0.06), thee (0.02), thy (0.10), thyself (0.06), unto (0.22) |
| – | 1968 | scriptures (0.02), isaiah (0.02), bringeth (0.009) |
| – | 1972 | scripture (0.03) |
| – | 1976 | – |
| – | 1980 | commandment (0.03) |
| – | from 1984 to 1996 | – |
| – | 2004 | samaritan (0.08), scripture (0.04) |
| – | 2008 | scripture (0.01), moses (0.09), joshua (0.13), mountaintop (0.02) |

to draw on scriptural language and produce overt biblical references. No such statistically salient tendency has been found in the GOP camp.

To the best of my knowledge, this Democratic Party-leaning trend has never been discovered nor accounted for in the literature. Also, it qualifies as one of the most counterintuitive patterns unearthed in this research as it contradicts conventional wisdom, which would most certainly attribute such a trend to a rather recent Republican Party. Not only does it question conventional wisdom, but it actually goes so far as to contradict claims made by specialists of religion and politics.

Berlinerblau (2008: 3–13), for example, describes the use of the Bible in politics as a mostly Republican tendency triggered by the 1973 *Roe v. Wade* case and by the ensuing comeback of the evangelicals in politics in favor of the GOP. The only real exception to this tendency that Berlinerblau is ready to concede is not to be found in former history—his Bible comeback model implying a near disappearance thereof during the first three quarters of the twentieth century—but in the appropriate rhetorical readjustment initiated by the last Democratic Party frontrunners as a necessary response to the 2004 religious fiasco experienced by candidate John Kerry.

It almost sounds like an understatement to say that our data-driven findings are far from supporting Berlinerblau's claims. Another challenge to his theory lies not so much in the rhetoric of the Democratic Party but in the absence—in Table 4.4—of any salient biblical item in the GOP camp.

Admittedly, there is still the possibility of viewing the Bible pattern discovered here as a validation of the "Scripture game" rules laid out by Berlinerblau, who believes that a specific way of using the Bible is politically effective. He says: "To the would-be candidate who wishes to bring the Bible into his or her rhetoric, I have just counseled keeping it (1) sparse, (2) positive, (3) vague, (4) shallow, and (5) veiled" (200: 83). Although we cannot subscribe to Berlinerblau's belief in the greater effectiveness of such biblical language without real evidence, we may remain tempted to trust him in his claim that some of the biblical language inserted in political rhetoric is vague, shallow and veiled. These qualities make such rhetoric more difficult to spot than biblical language that is overt or even verbatim. Consequently, this means that the Bible pattern observed in Table 4.4 may actually tell us more about the potential limitations of the methodology and tools employed in the present research than about a Democratic Party-specific trend. However, the real limitation is perhaps not in the methodology as such but in the kind of inferences that one is willing to make. It seems fair to say that the Bible pattern indicates a higher tendency among Democratic Party candidates to produce unveiled biblical language, but it is wrong to claim that we have found evidence that proves that the Democratic Party has been the only one to engage in biblical language.

Of course—according to Berlinerblau's rationale—those who make good political use of the Bible are those who follow the Scripture game rules. If he is right about effective biblical language—which is not proven—this would mean that the Bible pattern in Table 4.4 might actually represent enduring bad usage of biblical references on the part of Democratic Party candidates. What Berlinerblau says about the biblical language of 2004 Democratic Party candidate Kerry is worth reading as it provides one illustration of what he considers to be bad biblical language:

> Kerry's scriptural sprinkles were conspicuous in the extreme. Every verse he cited seemed to spark a national referendum on his Scripture-citing technique. On March 28, 2004, Kerry appeared at an African American church in St. Louis and exclaimed, "The Scriptures say, 'What does it profit my brethren if some say he has faith but does not have works?' [Jas. 2:14]. When we look at what's happening in America today, where are the works of compassion? Because it's also written, 'Be doers of the word and not hearers only [Jas. 1:22].'" Verbatim quotes, I have suggested, are rarely a good idea. . . . That Kerry's use of Scripture was strained goes without saying.
>
> (Berlinerblau 2008: 91–92)

Conversely, Berlinerblau considers Clinton—along with George W. Bush—as a master of the Bible-citing craft (2008: 83). There is a striking and potentially revealing coincidence in the fact that the 1992 and 1996 corpus files for Clinton (Table 4.4) are not marked by any salient biblical item. At first sight, it might seem fair to posit that behind such coincidental statistical silence hides the possibility that Clinton mostly kept his biblical references sparse, vague, shallow and/or veiled (Ibid.). Given the presence of several salient scriptural items for the 2008 Democratic Party campaign (Table 4.4), the same coincidence vanishes for Obama, whom Berlinerblau nonetheless—and paradoxically—considers as having "the best Scripture game in town" (2008: 3).

Altogether, what we are mostly left with are incentives to dig deeper in order to better assess previous scholarly work like that of Berlinerblau and integrate our own findings into the picture. Any attempt to provide a definite answer as to how biblical language has worked its way into political rhetoric or to resolve the many conundrums posed by the tensions between our findings and Berlinerblau's claims is bound to take us well beyond the confines of corpus linguistic analyses, and therefore, well beyond our scope. There is however a much more realistic and quite necessary step that can be taken, i.e. that of providing more quantitative data in order to feed future research and debates with quantitative facts instead of mere intuitions and beliefs. I have tried to achieve this goal by means of four different but complementary analyses.

The first of these analyses was elicited by a specific passage (emphasized in the next quotation) from Berlinerblau's Bible-citing recommendations:

> My last recommendation for would-be speechwriters is to *conceal references*. . . . citing chapter and verse is generally a no-no. **The politician who opens with the words "As we read in Chronicles 2:14 . . ."** is running a variety of risks.
>
> (Berlinerblau 2008: 82 [emphasis mine])

The above recommendation fed the desire to track exactly that kind of "bibliography-style" references. Another concomitant analysis was triggered by observing the results of Table 4.4 and realizing that overt references to or from the Bible seemed more present in the Democratic Party camp. This second analysis consists in a mere query for the word *bible* and potential derivations and synonyms. The third analysis aims to detect verbatim quotes from the Bible. Finally, the fourth analysis expands upon the rationale of this third analysis and seeks to spot verbatim quotes from another source than the Bible, i.e. from the most common Christian hymns. Each of these four analyses was conducted in the PCS corpus.

### 4.3.1. *Analysis 1*

In order to identify the unconcealed bibliography-style openings which Berlinerblau recommends against (Berlinerblau 2008: 82), a specific search list was devised from the table of contents provided in the Project Gutenberg version of the King James Bible (Figure 4.4).

Quite logically, a query that would aim to build an exhaustive list of the explicit bibliography-style references to the Bible should integrate every element of Figure 4.4. However, some of these elements came with the unpleasant promise of long hours of cleaning away false positive results. This is notably the case with quite common words like *job, judges, numbers, acts, john, matthew, mark* or *luke*. The choice was therefore made to take an easier course and remove such elements from the search list. The result is the following 41-node-long search list, out of an initial number of 57 different nodes that could have been included in the query: *genesis/ chronicles/exodus/ezra/hosea/leviticus/nehemiah/amos/deuteronomy/ obadiah/joshua/psalms/jonah/proverbs/micah/ruth/ecclesiastes/nahum/ solomon/habakkuk/isaiah/zephaniah/kings/jeremiah/haggai/lamentations/zechariah/ezekiel/malachi/ephesians/hebrews/philippians/colossians/thessalonians/romans/corinthians/titus/jude/galatians/philemon/ revelation*

There is no need to say that arbitrarily selecting elements from a list that contains other equally important results introduces an undeniable limitation to our analysis. It should also be noted that 2 among the 41 nodes

| | The Project Gutenberg Edition of the King James Bible | | | | | | |
|---|---|---|---|---|---|---|---|
| 77 | | | | | | | |
| 78 | | | | | | | |
| 79 | | | | | | | |
| 80 | Table Of Contents | | | | | | |
| 81 | | | | | | | |
| 82 | Book 01 | Genesis | Book 14 | 2 Chronicles | Book 27 | Daniel | |
| 83 | Book 02 | Exodus | Book 15 | Ezra | Book 28 | Hosea | |
| 84 | Book 03 | Leviticus | Book 16 | Nehemiah | Book 29 | Joel | |
| 85 | Book 04 | Numbers | Book 17 | Esther | Book 30 | Amos | |
| 86 | Book 05 | Deuteronomy | Book 18 | Job | Book 31 | Obadiah | |
| 87 | Book 06 | Joshua | Book 19 | Psalms | Book 32 | Jonah | |
| 88 | Book 07 | Judges | Book 20 | Proverbs | Book 33 | Micah | |
| 89 | Book 08 | Ruth | Book 21 | Ecclesiastes | Book 34 | Nahum | |
| 90 | Book 09 | 1 Samuel | Book 22 | Song of Solomon | Book 35 | Habakkuk | |
| 91 | Book 10 | 2 Samuel | Book 23 | Isaiah | Book 36 | Zephaniah | |
| 92 | Book 11 | 1 Kings | Book 24 | Jeremiah | Book 37 | Haggai | |
| 93 | Book 12 | 2 Kings | Book 25 | Lamentations | Book 38 | Zechariah | |
| 94 | Book 13 | 1 Chronicles | Book 26 | Ezekiel | Book 39 | Malachi | |
| 95 | | | | | | | |
| 96 | Book 40 | Matthew | Book 49 | Ephesians | Book 58 | Hebrews | |
| 97 | Book 41 | Mark | Book 50 | Philippians | Book 59 | James | |
| 98 | Book 42 | Luke | Book 51 | Colossians | Book 60 | 1 Peter | |
| 99 | Book 43 | John | Book 52 | 1 Thessalonians | Book 61 | 2 Peter | |
| 100 | Book 44 | Acts | Book 53 | 2 Thessalonians | Book 62 | 1 John | |
| 101 | Book 45 | Romans | Book 54 | 1 Timothy | Book 63 | 2 John | |
| 102 | Book 46 | 1 Corinthians | Book 55 | 2 Timothy | Book 64 | 3 John | |
| 103 | Book 47 | 2 Corinthians | Book 56 | Titus | Book 65 | Jude | |
| 104 | Book 48 | Galatians | Book 57 | Philemon | Book 66 | Revelation | |

*Figure 4.4* Table of contents of the Project Gutenberg Edition of the King James Bible

above—namely *isaiah* and *joshua*—are part of the salient items of Table 4.4. We must, therefore, be aware of the overlap that there will be between the pattern returned from the upcoming analysis and Table 4.4.

Reducing the search list down to 41 items did not prevent undesirable results from occurring. Among the 181 matches that the 41-node search list initially returned from the PCS corpus, no fewer than 104 hits (i.e. 57.46%) were identified—via concordance reading—as false positive results. Otherwise stated, this means that 77 hits (i.e. 42.54%) were identified as unconcealed biblical references of the kind that Berlinerblau recommends against.

Table 4.5 reports the 77 valid results onto the time and party lines. The bracketed values correspond to the raw frequencies (i.e. number of hits) produced by the candidates.

Table 4.5 calls for several comments. The first one concerns its undeniable tendency towards the Democratic Party. Out of the 27 files contained in the PCS corpus, 17 files (62.96%) are marked by at least one of the 41 nodes. In the Democratic Party camp, the proportion of files that are marked by one node or more rises up to 92.86%, and only the 1976 Democratic Party file remains unmarked by any of the 41 nodes. Conversely, the proportion of GOP files that are marked by one node or more falls to a 30.77% score, with only 4 files out of 13 containing at least one of the 41 nodes.

*Table 4.5* Pattern returned from analysis 1: identifying the unconcealed bibliography-style openings in the PCS corpus (N = raw frequencies)

| Republican Party | Year | Democratic Party |
|---|---|---|
| ecclesiastes (2) | 1952 | jeremiah (1) |
| – | 1956 | amos (1) |
| isaiah (1) | 1960 | solomon (1), isaiah (2) |
| no 1964 GOP file | 1964 | isaiah (15) |
| – | 1968 | isaiah (7), amos (1) |
| – | 1972 | isaiah (3), micah (1) |
| – | 1976 | – |
| psalms (2) | 1980 | exodus (1) |
| – | 1984 | isaiah (1) |
| – | 1988 | isaiah (1) |
| – | 1992 | isaiah (1) |
| proverbs (1) | 1996 | proverbs (1), nehemiah (1) |
| – | 2004 | hebrews (2) |
| – | 2008 | deuteronomy (1), joshua (28), corinthians (1), amos (1) |

Table 4.5 adds to the pattern observed in Table 4.4. The cumulative effect that we get from the superposition of both tables undeniably suggests the existence of a Democratic Party-specific feature. However, the raw frequencies observed in Table 4.5 also attest to the rarity and "low-profile" nature that are inherent to many constitutive parts of this party-specific trend. Consequently, this trend may appear of little quantitative significance, and this in spite of the fact that comparing the party-specific aggregate frequencies obtained from Table 4.5 returns a statistically significant difference (Democratic Party aggregate frequency: 71 hits or 0.02 per 1,000 words; GOP aggregate frequency: 6 hits or 0.002 per 1,000 words. $x^2=38.13737$, difference is significant at $p < 0.001$).

### 4.3.2. *Analysis 2*

As explained earlier, Table 4.4 seems to indicate that overall, the Democratic Party candidates have produced overt biblical references more frequently and more recurrently than their GOP counterparts. A thorough investigation into each item of Table 4.4 was seen as beyond the scope of the present research. However, we can narrow down the scope of research to the main idea probably suggested by Table 4.4, which can be put in general terms as follows: the Bible seems to have been more present in the Democratic Party's campaign rhetoric than in the GOP's. In turn, this observation calls for tracking down references to the Bible itself. To do so, the query *scriptur\*/bible/bibles/biblical/biblically/good book/old testament/ new testament/holy writ* was run across all the files of the PCS corpus. The query returned 196 hits: 48 hits for *scriptur\** (24.49%), 91 hits for *bible* (46.43%), 27 hits for *biblical* (13.78%), 13 hits for *good book* (6.63%), 12 hits for *old testament* (6.12%) and 5 hits for *new testament* (2.55%). Reading through the concordance lines helped identify 12 false positive results that had to be discarded.

Table 4.6—which reports the 184 valid hits (and their raw frequencies) on the time and party spectra—indicates that the most unconcealed biblical references one can probably think of have been predominantly produced by the Democratic Party candidates. The raw frequencies in Table 4.6 suggest that most Democratic candidates produced these biblical items on rare occasions, while a few others—most notably Kennedy (1960), Johnson (1964), McGovern (1972) and Carter (1976)—drew more heavily on them (with aggregate relative frequencies of 0.07, 0.10, 0.07 and 0.07 respectively). Once again, comparing the party-specific aggregate frequencies of Table 4.6 returns a statistically significant difference favoring the Democratic Party camp (Democratic Party aggregate frequency: 146 hits or 0.04 per 1,000 words; GOP aggregate frequency: 38 hits or 0.01 per 1,000 words. $x^2=37.56891$, difference is significant at $p < 0.001$).

*Table 4.6* Pattern returned from analysis 2: tracking down references to the Bible in the PCS corpus (query *scriptur\*/bible/bibles/biblical/biblically/good book/old testament/new testament/holy writ*; N = raw frequencies)

| Republican Party | Year | Democratic Party |
|---|---|---|
| bible (4), old testament (1) | 1952 | scriptur* (1), bible (3), biblical (3), old testament (1) |
| bible (1), biblical (1) | 1956 | bible (1) |
| – | 1960 | scriptur* (3), bible (22), biblical (3), old testament (1) |
| no 1964 GOP file | 1964 | scriptur* (2), bible (10), biblical (1), good book (12), old testament (1) |
| – | 1968 | scriptur* (13), bible (1), old testament (2) |
| bible (1) | 1972 | scriptur* (6), bible (3), biblical (1), new testament (2) |
| bible (8), old testament (1), new testament (1) | 1976 | bible (3), biblical (3), old testament (1), new testament (1) |
| scriptur* (2), biblical (1) | 1980 | bible (4), old testament (1), new testament (1) |
| bible (6) | 1984 | bible (2), biblical (3) |
| bible (1) | 1988 | scriptur* (1), old testament (2) |
| biblical (9) | 1992 | scriptur* (5), bible (1), old testament (1) |
| – | 1996 | scriptur* (2), bible (3) |
| – | 2004 | scriptur* (5), bible (3) |
| bible (1) | 2008 | scriptur* (8), bible (2), biblical (2) |

### 4.3.3. Analyses 3 and 4

The third analysis aims to extend the scope of investigations beyond the word unit level. To do so, it was decided to track down 7-word-long verbatim sequences—henceforth called 7-grams—that were drawn from the Bible and inserted into campaign speeches. To the best of my knowledge, this constitutes an unprecedented attempt at measuring the extent to which presidential candidates have quoted verbatim from the Bible. At the outset, it is important to recognize that the 7-word-long cutoff is arbitrarily chosen and is a minimal necessary requirement for any verbatim quote to be spotted. Such cutoff means that any quoted sequence that fails to line up at least 7 words verbatim from the Bible will remain undetected. The same is of course not true for verbatim sequences that contain more than 7 words, in which case several 7-grams would logically point towards the same biblical passage. This is perfectly illustrated in Figure 4.5, where two 7-grams (i.e. *time to keep and a time to* and *to keep and a time to cast*) point to the same

| 2 | "A Season for Everything." In that chapter there is a sentence, "A time to keep and a time to cast away." That is a good text for this |
| 3 | do to doubt that America can still be a land of great miracles. This is a time to keep and a time to cast away. One of the first things we will |
| 4 | is found in the Book of Ecclesiastes that reads: "There is ... a time to keep and a time to cast away." This is a time to cast away |
| 5 | any area vital to our welfare. In the words of our text, "There is a time to keep and a time to cast away." Now is the time for both. The |
| 6 | "A Season for Everything." In that chapter there is a sentence, "A time to keep and a time to cast away." That is a good text for this political |
| 7 | doubt that America can still be a land of great miracles. This is a time to keep and a time to cast away. One of the first things we will cast |
| 8 | is found in the Book of Ecclesiastes that reads: "There is ... a time to keep and a time to cast away." This is a time to cast away some |
| 9 | any area vital to our welfare. In the words of our text, "There is a time to keep and a time to cast away." Now is the time for both. The |

*Figure 4.5* Two different 7-grams pointing towards a same biblical verbatim passage (Ecclesiastes 3:6) in Eisenhower's 1952 presidential campaign rhetoric

biblical passage (i.e. Ecclesiastes 3:6), which candidate Eisenhower used four times within two different speeches.

It is therefore easy to understand that the longer the verbatim quote, the larger the number of 7-grams that boil down to the same biblical passage. So, if a candidate should utter the following sequence (Figure 4.6)—which contains 12 words from the Bible—six 7-grams would help detect the same 12-word-long sequence, provided the Bible has been *exhaustively* sliced into 7-gram pieces and each of these pieces inserted into an exhaustive search list.

Slicing the Bible into N-grams as those presented in Figure 4.6 is something that *WordSmith* can accomplish provided one has a .txt version of the Bible at hand (for a discussion of the settings adopted for this N-gram detection, see Vincent 2014: 297–299). The choice was therefore made to download the complete King James Bible from the Project Gutenberg website (for a discussion of this choice, see Vincent 2014: 295). This implies that departure from our own set of verbatim 7-grams may happen in different ways. It may be caused by the production of a non-verbatim quote or else by the production of a verbatim quote from another version of the King James Bible or from another translation of the Bible entirely.

Other limitations also get in the way of an exhaustive detection of biblical passages, even those that are verbatim. One such limitation is caused by the very choice to work with 7-word-long sequences. As stated earlier, it is quite easy to understand that any verbatim quote that contains fewer than 7 words will remain undetected by the 7-gram analysis. Such shorter verbatim quotes have been used by candidates and are present in our PCS corpus. Some of them were detected while working on other unreported analyses (Vincent 2014). One such passage was for example detected while analyzing how the biblical reference *isaiah* was used by 1964 candidate Johnson, who said "[W]e can . . . follow the advice of the prophet Isaiah, 'Come now, *let us reason together.*'" (Johnson, September 17, 1964. "Remarks on Conservations at a Breakfast in Portland", emphasis mine). The 4-word-long sequence *let us reason together*—which occurs 10 times in the 1964 Democratic Party file—is a verbatim sequence from the Bible, which reads "Come now, and *let us reason together*" (Isaiah 1:18, emphasis mine). Had

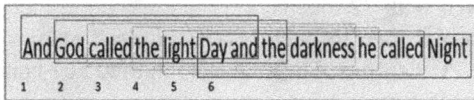

*Figure 4.6* The six possible 7-grams in a 12-word-long sequence

Johnson produced the 7-word-long verbatim sequence *come now and let us reason together*, our 7-gram analysis would have detected it, all the more so if asking the *WordSmith* tools to ignore punctuation marks. Through this specific instance, we can see how even the slightest departure from the biblical source—i.e. the omission of *"and"* by Johnson—renders a sequence undetectable by our analysis. Also, this illustrates the advantage of working with shorter N-grams, as a 4-gram analysis would normally have detected the 4-word-long sequence *let us reason together*. But even a 4-gram analysis would miss the still shorter verbatim biblical passages that are also present in our corpus. Bill Clinton for instance produced one such passage when he said, "Let us build a nation that our seed will honor as long as the sun and *the moon endureth*" (Clinton, B., September 9, 1992. "B'nai B'rith International Convention speech", Washington D.C., emphasis mine). The 3-word-long sequence *the moon endureth* is a verbatim quote from the Psalms 72:7 "In his days shall the righteous flourish; and abundance of peace so long as *the moon endureth*" (emphasis mine). It is easy to understand that only a 3-gram analysis would have detected such a biblical passage.

Based on all this, it seems fair to question the choice to work with 7-grams only. There are however several reasons that justify the decision to use 7-grams. First, slicing the Bible into smaller sequences would have resulted in longer search lists to run on *Concord*. Such longer search lists would have required more computer resources and more work to validate and identify the results with a precise biblical reference. These longer search lists were deemed as beyond feasibility. They were discarded also because many among the shorter N-grams run the risk of being less Bible specific. Longer sequences therefore appeared more appealing, although probably more exposed to the danger posed by any kind of departure from the Biblical source. Being aware of such danger fed the desire to strike a good balance, hence the choice for 7-word-long clusters. *WordSmith* sliced the Bible into 574,083 such clusters. Parenthetically but interestingly, this figure corresponds to the number of every unique 7-gram type identified by *WordSmith*, not the total number of 7-gram tokens found, which is larger. Among the 574,083 7-gram types indexed by *WordSmith*, the first 20,390 types occur more than once, meaning that each one of them materializes into several tokens. Likewise, the observed frequency for the first 284 7-gram types amounts to 10 tokens or more. The most frequently observed 7-gram type is /AND THE LORD SPAKE UNTO MOSES SAYING/ with 72 tokens.

The next step was then to query every single 7-gram—via *Concord*—across the entire PCS corpus. The analysis returned 567 concordance lines. A sample is given in Figure 4.7.

The 567 concordance lines were analyzed, and the 7-gram matches validated or else discarded accordingly. Every valid 7-gram was associated with its corresponding biblical twin and further described through details provided on the Annenberg/Pew Archive database (e.g. candidate, date, description, type of speech, city, state). This identification procedure was necessary to avoid counting the same verbatim passage more than once. Also, it helped make possible a precise count of the number of speeches containing the verbatim passages and helped us calculate the percentage—per candidate—that such speeches represent when compared to the total number of speeches contained in the PCS corpus files. Such values are reported in Table 4.7 (see column "in N speeches"). The bracketed values in Table 4.7 account for the 7-word-long passages that could not be validated as verbatim quotes with absolute certainty.[15] These passages are tagged with the /?/ symbol in Table 4.7. Also in Table 4.7, one can read that the biblical passages found in campaign rhetoric are reported in the form of biblical references like [Luke 23:34]. Each reference counts for one verbatim passage. In some cases, a candidate uses the same verbatim quote more than just once. For instance, 1964 Democratic Party candidate Johnson referred to [Luke 23:34] on two different occasions, hence the fact that Table 4.7 contains two entries to [Luke 23:34] for the 1964 Democratic Party campaign.

Although raw frequencies do not always guarantee the most solid comparisons, it is quite safe to claim that a Democratic-Party-leaning pattern stands out in Table 4.7. When compared to the GOP candidates—and with

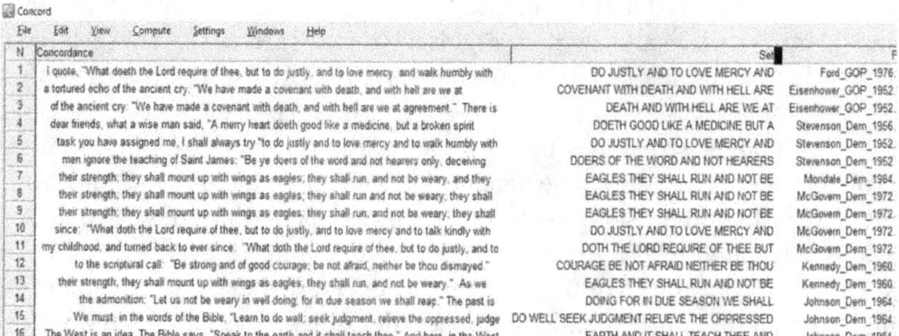


| N | Concordance | Set | F |
|---|---|---|---|
| 1 | i quote, "What doeth the Lord require of thee, but to do justly, and to love mercy and walk humbly with | DO JUSTLY AND TO LOVE MERCY AND | Ford_GOP_1976. |
| 2 | a tortured echo of the ancient cry: "We have made a covenant with death, and with hell are we at | COVENANT WITH DEATH AND WITH HELL ARE | Eisenhower_GOP_1952. |
| 3 | of the ancient cry: "We have made a covenant with death, and with hell are we at agreement." There is | DEATH AND WITH HELL ARE WE AT | Eisenhower_GOP_1952. |
| 4 | dear friends, what a wise man said, "A merry heart doeth good like a medicine, but a broken spirit | DOETH GOOD LIKE A MEDICINE BUT A | Stevenson_Dem_1956. |
| 5 | task you have assigned me, I shall always try "to do justly and to love mercy and to walk humbly with | DO JUSTLY AND TO LOVE MERCY AND | Stevenson_Dem_1952. |
| 6 | men ignore the teaching of Saint James: "Be ye doers of the word and not hearers only, deceiving | DOERS OF THE WORD AND NOT HEARERS | Stevenson_Dem_1952 |
| 7 | their strength; they shall mount up with wings as eagles; they shall run, and not be weary, and they | EAGLES THEY SHALL RUN AND NOT BE | Mondale_Dem_1984. |
| 8 | their strength; they shall mount up with wings as eagles; they shall run and not be weary; they shall | EAGLES THEY SHALL RUN AND NOT BE | McGovern_Dem_1972. |
| 9 | their strength; they shall mount up with wings as eagles; they shall run, and not be weary; they shall | EAGLES THEY SHALL RUN AND NOT BE | McGovern_Dem_1972. |
| 10 | since: "What doth the Lord require of thee, but to do justly, and to love mercy and to talk kindly with | DO JUSTLY AND TO LOVE MERCY AND | McGovern_Dem_1972. |
| 11 | my childhood, and turned back to ever since: "What doth the Lord require of thee, but to do justly, and to | DOTH THE LORD REQUIRE OF THEE BUT | McGovern_Dem_1972. |
| 12 | to the scriptural call: "Be strong and of good courage; be not afraid, neither be thou dismayed." | COURAGE BE NOT AFRAID NEITHER BE THOU | Kennedy_Dem_1960. |
| 13 | their strength, they shall mount up with wings as eagles, they shall run, and not be weary." As we | EAGLES THEY SHALL RUN AND NOT BE | Kennedy_Dem_1960. |
| 14 | the admonition: "Let us not be weary in well doing: for in due season we shall reap." The past is | DOING FOR IN DUE SEASON WE SHALL | Johnson_Dem_1964. |
| 15 | . We must, in the words of the Bible, "Learn to do well; seek judgment, relieve the oppressed, judge | DO WELL SEEK JUDGMENT RELIEVE THE OPPRESSED | Johnson_Dem_1964. |
| 16 | . The West is an idea. The Bible says, "Speak to the earth and it shall teach thee." And here, in the West, | EARTH AND IT SHALL TEACH THEE AND | Johnson_Dem_1964. |
| 17 | to every purpose under the Heaven--"a time to break down, and a time to build up." Well, I believe that | DOWN AND A TIME TO BUILD UP | Johnson_Dem_1964. |
| 18 | , end poverty and famine, provide education. "The desert shall rejoice--and blossom as the rose." This | DESERT SHALL REJOICE AND BLOSSOM AS THE | Humphrey_Dem_1968. |

*Figure 4.7* Screenshot of concordance lines returned from the Bible-specific 7-gram search list in the PCS Corpus

Table 4.7 Results returned from the 7-gram detection—in the PCS corpus—of verbatim passages from the Bible (analysis 3)

| Republican Party | | | | Democratic Party | | | | |
|---|---|---|---|---|---|---|---|---|
| Total N Speeches | in N Speeches | N. Verbatim quotes | Verbatim Quotes from: | Year | Verbatim Quotes from: | N. verbatim quotes | in N speeches | total N speeches |
| 230 | 3 1.30% | 6 | Ecclesiastes 3:6; Ecclesiastes 3:6; Ecclesiastes 3:6; Ecclesiastes 3:6; Isaiah 28:15; Psalms 55:21 | 1952 | James 1:22; Jeremiah 6:14 /?/; Luke 12:48; Matthew 6:33; Matthew 7:21; Matthew 16:26; Matthew 26:42; Micah 6:8; Psalms 23:4 /?/; Psalms 121:1 | 8 (+2?) | 7 (+2) 3.76% (4.84%) | 186 |
| 43 | (1) (2.33%) | (1?) | Jeremiah 34:18–19 /?/ | 1956 | Jeremiah 6:14 /?/; Matthew 7:20; Proverbs 17:22; Zechariah 4:6 | 3 (+1?) | 3 (+1) 4% (5.33%) | 75 |
| 136 | 1 0.74% | 1 | Isaiah 2:4 | 1960 | Deuteronomy 30:13; Galatians 6:7; Isaiah 40:31; Joshua 1:9; Matthew 6:24; Matthew 25:35–36; Psalms 55:21 | 7 | 6 1.92% | 312 |
| — | — | — | no 1964 GOP file | 1964 | Corinthians(1) 3:13; Deuteronomy 15:11; Ecclesiastes 1:4; Ecclesiastes 3:1; Ephesians 4:14; Galatians 6:9; Hebrews 12:1; Isaiah 1:17; Isaiah 1:18; James 1:19; Job 12:8; Job 38:7; Luke 11:21; Luke 23:34; Matthew 7:24–25; Proverbs 16:32 | 17 | 12 10.81% | 111 |
| 58 | 0 | 0 | ∅ | 1968 | Isaiah 35:1; Isaiah 52:7; Isaiah 52:7; Isaiah 52:7; Matthew 16:26; Psalms 23:4 /?/; Psalms 121:1 | 7 (+1?) | 6 3.92% | 153 |

(Continued)

Table 4.7 (Continued)

| Republican Party | | | Democratic Party | | | | |
|---|---|---|---|---|---|---|---|
| Total N Speeches | N. Verbatim in N Speeches quotes | Verbatim Quotes from: | Year | Verbatim Quotes from: | N. verbatim quotes | in N speeches | total N speeches |
| 59 | 0 / 0 | Ø | 1972 | Chronicles (2) 7 :14 Deuteronomy 30:19; Deuteronomy 30:19; Ecclesiastes 3:1; Isaiah 40:31; Isaiah 40:31; Luke 4:18; Mark 8:36; Micah, 6:8; Proverbs 29:18 | 12 | 10 10.20% | 98 |
| 128 | 2 1.56% / 2 | Micah 6:8; Romans 14:19 | 1976 | Corinthians (1) 14:8; Isaiah 2:4; Matthew 7:1 | 3 | 3 5.45% | 55 |
| 69 | 1 1.45% / 1 | Matthew 28:19 | 1980 | Matthew 7:1 | 1 | 1 1.12% | 89 |
| 108 | 0 / 0 | Ø | 1984 | Isaiah 40:31; Matthew 7:20 | 2 | 2 3.03% | 66 |
| 41 | 0 / 0 | Ø | 1988 | Isaiah 61:3; Peter (1) 1:22; Peter (1) 1:22; Peter (1) 1:22 | 4 | 3 4.55% | 66 |
| 126 | 0 / 0 | Ø | 1992 | Proverbs 29:18; Proverbs 29:18 | 2 | 2 1.32% | 76 |
| 78 | 1 (+1) 1.28% (2.56%) / 1 (+1?) | Proverbs 3:5–6; Psalms 23:4 /?/ | 1996 | Proverbs 22:6 | 1 | 1 0.90% | 111 |
| 39 | 0 / 0 | Ø | 2004 | Hebrews 11:1; Hebrews 11:1; Psalms 19:14 | 3 | 2 3.45% | 58 |
| 143 | 0 / 0 | Ø | 2008 | Corinthians (1) 13:11; Joshua 1:3; Matthew, 7: 24–25 | 3 | 3 1.70% | 176 |

the exception of the 1980 and 1996 campaigns—there has been a higher tendency among the 1952–2008 Democratic Party candidates to insert 7-word-long (or longer) verbatim passages into their campaign rhetoric. Such a tendency must, however, be qualified as quite rare, as attested by the fairly low raw frequencies observed and by the similarly low proportions of speeches (expressed in % values in Table 4.7) that contain the verbatim sequences. Several candidates—most notably Johnson 1964 and McGovern 1972—score higher percentage points than others, which may lead to some interesting questions for future research, all the more so as these candidates have been somewhat neglected in the literature on religious rhetoric.

Although quantitatively rare, the verbatim passages that have been found via the 7-gram analysis form another interesting pattern that also contradicts conventional wisdom and poses a conundrum if one considers the statistics reported by Wilcox and Fortelny:

> [A]mong the core of the Christian Right, 92 percent believe in an iner-rant or literal Bible, and 91 percent think that Jesus is the only path to salvation. . . . [A]mong the religious Left core, only 33 percent think that the Bible is inerrant or literally true, whereas only 45 percent believe that Jesus is the only path to salvation.
>
> (Wilcox and Fortelny 2009: 290)

It is quite intriguing to see that the party that is traditionally associated with those described as less inclined to believe in an inerrant or literal Bible is paradoxically the one which has produced the largest amount of biblical references, at least in our corpus. The relative scarcity of verbatim quotes found in the GOP camp and the Christian Right's propensity to believe in an inerrant or literal Bible offers another quite intriguing paradox.

This paradox led me to postulate the presence of passages quoted verba-tim from sources other than the Bible and hypothetically more accessible to those people siding with the Christian Right. The choice was therefore made to create a corpus of the most common Christian hymns in order to comple-ment the findings returned from the 7-gram analysis and run a similar kind of analysis in our PCS corpus. The exact same settings as those employed for the 7-gram analysis were adopted, with one notable exception, however: to wit, the cluster size set at 4 rather than 7 since the Christian hymns corpus is rather small and makes shorter N-gram detection manageable.

My corpus of Christian hymns was built along the same classification as that used on the *Hymnary.org* website (www.hymnary.org/browse/popular), which provides a list of the "hymns published the most frequently in modern hymnals indexed by Hymnary.org" (Ibid.). At the time of writing, my Chris-tian Hymn corpus contains all of the 242 hymns referenced on the *Hymnary. org* website and amounts to 32,994 running words. As implied above, this corpus was exhaustively sliced into 4-word-long sequences (4-grams). The resulting list contains 26,644 4-grams. All of them were searched for in the PCS corpus. Table 4.8 plots—on the time and party lines—the results of this combined query by providing the title of the hymn from which the verbatim 4-word-long quote was drawn as well as the exact date of utterance.

Once again, the Democratic-Party-leaning pattern returned is striking and counterintuitive, although it seems equally important to insist on the presence of only a limited number of instances drawn from a tiny fraction of the hymns contained in the corpus. Also—and with the exception of the Lord's Prayer instance in the Obama file—all the hymns contained in Table 4.8 seem highly civil religious in tone. It does not sound unreasonable to posit that these hymns actually indicate a higher tendency on the part of the Democratic Party candidates to draw from certain civil religious sources rather than from Christian hymns per se. A corpus linguistic approach focusing more precisely on the civil religious rhetoric inserted into political discourse might be an interesting path to explore in the future. Finally, one might be equally puzzled at the absence of results on the GOP side (with the exception of the 1984 campaign). All in all, our analysis of Bible-specific and hymn-specific language has thus revealed a very scarce

*Table 4.8* Pattern returned from analysis 4: detecting 4-grams from Christian hymns in the PCS corpus

| Republican Party | Year | Democratic Party |
|---|---|---|
| – | 1952 | "Battle Hymn of the Republic" (08/10/1952) |
| – | 1956 | – |
| – | 1960 | – |
| no 1964 GOP file | 1964 | "America the Beautiful" (31/10/1964) |
| – | 1968 | – |
| – | 1972 | "There is a Balm in Gilead" (04/09/1972) |
| – | 1976 | – |
| – | 1980 | "There is a Balm in Gilead" (20/10/1980) |
| "America the Beautiful" (20/09/1984) | 1984 | "America the Beautiful" (19/07/1984) + (29/09/1984) + (15/10/1984) "Battle Hymn of the Republic" (01/11/1984) |
| – | 1988 | "America the Beautiful" (01/10/1988) |
| – | 1992 | – |
| – | 1996 | – |
| – | 2004 | "Amazing Grace!" (09/09/2004) "America the Beautiful" (12/08/2004) |
| – | 2008 | "The Lord's Prayer/Our Father" (05/06/2007) "America the Beautiful" (08/01/2008) |

usage of such references by GOP candidates—at least in their general election campaign speeches—which pales in comparison with the cumulative pattern of usage found in the Democratic Party camp.

## Further Discussion and Concluding Remarks on the Bible Pattern

As argued above, the cumulative pattern obtained from the initial Bible pattern (Table 4.4) and from the four concomitant data-driven analyses is unmistakable, counterintuitive and, therefore, ripe with methodological lessons to draw, potential research questions to explore and conclusions to address. However, this cumulative pattern does not allow anyone to conclude that there has been a total absence of biblical language in the GOP camp. Although Berlinerblau's book poses questions as much as it brings answers, it provides valuable insights into the different ways politicians may exploit biblical language. These insights are all the more welcome as they provide likely examples of biblical references that would probably remain difficult to spot with common corpus linguistic techniques. In addition to broadening the scope of possibilities regarding biblical references, Berlinerblau's analyses suggest that the GOP camp has also inserted biblical references into its rhetoric. In what follows, we will consider what Berlinerblau says about such biblical language in George W. Bush's rhetoric. We will take advantage of these quotations to offer a few additional—and concluding—comments around Berlinerblau's analyses.

In the quotation below, we can read how he summarizes Bush's biblical language and describes it as being in line with the rules of effective Bible-citing:

> When reading through George W. Bush's seven State of the Union addresses and two inaugurals, it becomes apparent that he usually observes all of the aforementioned protocols. [W]hen the Bible is called upon, the quotes are integrated seamlessly and stealthily into the flow of ideas. . . . Bush rarely puts his adversaries on alert by citing chapter and verse. He never justifies a particular policy prescription by reference to a given text. His invocations are never set in acrimonious terms but offered as a means of celebrating the republic's finest virtues. And in terms of our criteria of shallowness he excels here as well. . . . Bush's speechwriters like to employ short phrases or clauses or snippets from the Bible, as opposed to entire verses.
>
> (Berlinerblau 2008: 83–84)

In Berlinerblau's view, Bush abides by the rules that make Bible citing politically effective. And since Bush's biblical language is most of the time in stealth mode—at least in Berlinerblau's opinion—there is little doubt that such language will not be detected as easily as overt biblical references. Once again, the above-quoted analysis needs qualification however. Indeed, one must be aware of the potential limitation that is induced by the very nature of the speeches on which Berlinerblau bases his account. It is generally agreed that Inaugurals and State of the Union addresses qualify as highly ritualized events for which the presence of non-partisan civil religious rhetoric is expected and actually quite the norm (Beasley 2004; Teten 2003: 336). The fact that Bush's biblical invocations in his Inaugural and State of the Union addresses serve to celebrate the virtues of the nation (Berlinerblau 2008: 84) and not to anger or alienate his opponents might in fact tell us more about the constraints of the genres than it does about Bush's rhetorical strategies. Although they can enlighten our understanding of the civil religious rhetoric that a president is expected to produce, such speeches are probably too narrowly constrained by genre and context-specific rules to permit our drawing conclusions regarding the entire biblical style of a president. Likewise, Inaugurals and State of the Union addresses only offer limited—and even potentially deceptive—insights when it comes to comparisons with campaign speeches like the ones produced by Kerry, which Berlinerblau uses to illustrate bad Bible-citing.

It would not be fair to Berlinerblau, however, if we kept silent about the few illustrations that he gives of Bush's breaking the rule to keep biblical references concealed (2008: 84–85). These examples are speeches that Bush delivered in the direct aftermath of the 9/11 attacks and which contained quotations from and references to the Bible. Although Berlinerblau defines such a particular time as "one exceptional moment in American history", it is regrettable that he remains silent about the possibility that Bush's overt biblical references were imposed by the post 9/11 mourning context more than by Bush's own rhetorical preferences. The possibility is that Bush played the much expected and quite traditional role of "High Priest" of civil religion (Bass and Rozell 2009: 481) more than that of an expert of politically effective biblical language.

As already argued, the illustrations of biblical language presented in Berlinerblau's work are valuable because they exemplify the various forms that biblical language can take and illustrate why some of this language may remain difficult to identify. In the excerpt below, Berlinerblau provides some interesting—albeit debatable (see for e.g. Olsen 2004)—examples and interpretations of biblically rooted passages inserted in Bush's Inaugural and State of the Union addresses:

> Thus, in his 2004 State of the Union address Bush exclaimed, "The same moral tradition that defines marriage also teaches us that each individual has dignity and value in God's sight." The phrase "God's

sight" appears a few times in standard English translations of the Old and New Testament. Bush seems to be shadowing 1 Peter 3:4: "Instead, it should be that of your inner self, the unfading beauty of a gentle and quiet spirit, which is of great worth in God's sight" (NIV). In his second Inaugural he reached into the Psalms (without, of course, ever mentioning the Psalms) and paid homage to "the Maker of Heaven and earth." ... [Bush's] 2001 State of the Union Address [is] virtually shorn of any biblical allusions save for the final words: "Together we can share in the credit of making our country more prosperous and generous and just, and earn from our conscience and from our fellow citizens the highest possible praise: Well done good and faithful servants." The reference to the faithful servant (from Matt. 25:21) would not go unnoticed by any literate Christian. As such, the president did not need to cue his listeners with a remark on the order of "As Matthew's Gospel teaches us . . ."

(Berlinerblau 2008: 84–85)

After identifying biblical references in Bush's rhetoric, Berlinerblau explains how such messages were received and comments on the political effectiveness of such rhetoric. The author is quite right when he reports that Bush's rhetoric "[has driven] his critics to distraction" (2008: 85) and that "commentators often lament the 'hidden passages,' 'double coding,' or 'winks and nudges' in his public communications" (Ibid.). However, a healthy dose of scepticism is permitted when it comes to Berlinerblau's unsubstantiated claim that "[n]o matter how much it may outrage pundits and scholars, this tactic is devastatingly effective" (Ibid.). Not only does he omit to provide any kind of evidence for such supposed effectiveness, but he grounds it in another belief, to wit, that "Bush's Christian supporters know Scripture like the backs of their hands" (Ibid.). Berlinerblau concludes as follows:

Accordingly, Bush can signal the base without raising the hackles of persnickety Establishment Clause purists. Indeed, nonbelievers in front of their television sets—who usually can't be bothered to think seriously about religion—continue munching away at their pretzels without having the faintest idea that the president has just communed with about a hundred million Americans. In so doing, Bush keeps the protestations of ACLU activists out of the next day's news cycle and often well beyond that.

(Berlinerblau 2008: 85)

The belief that the President can effectively send religiously laden coded signals to his political base is grounded in the unsubstantiated premise that "about a hundred million Americans" (Ibid.) are actually able to get such coded signals, contrary to pretzels-munching nonbelievers who are—in Berlinerblau's view—not even conscious of such religious communion. As further argued below, this premise of a biblically-well-versed voting bloc—which undergirds the resulting belief in the effectiveness of hidden religious language—should be confronted with the contrary evidence found in other scholarly research.

These findings—reported in Prothero (2007) and in the 2010 Pew Forum "U.S. Religious Knowledge Survey"—provide a measure of the religious knowledge of American people. If anything, it seems fair to say that they clearly challenge some of Berlinerblau's claims. For instance, the Pew Forum Survey announces that "[a]theists and agnostics, Jews and Mormons perform better than other groups on the survey even after controlling for different levels of education" (The Pew Forum on Religion & Public Life 2010: 6). In turn, these measures suggest that—contrary to the deprecating image drawn by Berlinerblau—there might be more that comes to the non-believers' ear than the mere sound of pretzel chewing after all. However, one should not be mistaken by the slightly better knowledge measured among these groups. Indeed—and provided Prothero is right—the main lesson that seems to come out from studies measuring religious knowledge is that of a widely shared illiteracy about religion, irrespective of the slightly better results scored by some groups. According to Prothero, "today it is a rare American who can follow with any degree of confidence biblically inflected debates about abortion or gay marriage. Or, for that matter, about the economy, since the most widely quoted Bible verse in the United States—'God helps those who help themselves'—is not actually in the Bible" (2007: 11). According to Prothero, such ignorance is all the more deplorable as it impinges on democracy itself, and this because of the place that religion occupies in the public square. Hence Prothero's rhetorical question: "In an era in which the public square is, rightly or wrongly, awash in religious reasons, can one really participate fully in public life without knowing something about Christianity and the world's religions?" (2007: 12).

## Notes

1. With a maximum p-value of 0.001 (min. frequency cutoff=3), *catholic* is a statistically salient keyword in six files out of the 12 1952–1996 Democratic Party files (i.e. in Stevenson [1952], Kennedy [1960], McGovern [1972], Carter [1976], Carter [1980] and Clinton [1992]). When using a less restrictive max. p-value of 0.01, *catholic* is also found salient in Humphrey (1968).
2. The query *catholic** returned 190 hits : 153 hits (80.53%) for *catholic*, 2 hits (1.05%) for *catholicism* and 35 hits (18.42%) for *catholics*.
3. The probability value obtained for the 2008 campaign could be rejected by many corpus linguists on the grounds that—as made clear by Granger and

Paquot—"[i]n corpus linguistics, the usual threshold is 0.01. Thus, for a $X^2$ to be significant, the p value must be equal to or smaller than 0.01" (Granger and Paquot 2010: 8–10).

4. Wilson (2007: 179) partially answers these questions while commenting on John Kerry's appeals to Catholics. He says: "John Kerry . . . often mentioned to Catholic audiences that he had been an altar boy . . . . 'Vote for me,' he seemed to say, 'because we share this sociological bond, because we have familiarity with the same religious rituals of childhood.' It was an appeal in the old style of group identity politics. And, as has been documented here and elsewhere, it fell flat."

5. Test result: $X^2 = 18.36297$. Difference is significant at $p < 0.001$. Clinton 1992: 27 hits out of 227,853 = 0.118 (relative frequency per 1,000); Clinton 1996: 8 hits out of 338,930 = 0.023 (relative frequency per 1,000).

6. The dispersion value accounts for the dispersion of a given node across a given file. The dispersion value ranges from 0 to 1. The closer to 1, the more evenly dispersed the node is throughout the file. A dispersion value that is closer to 0 indicates that the node is more isolated and limited to a few specific locations in the file.

7. We follow Hunston's advice to combine both tests to assess the statistical relationship between a node and its collocates (Hunston 2002: 69–75). The thresholds for the significance of the strength and certainty of the relationship are those defined and used by Hunston (Ibid.).

8. Sullivan's observation about McGovern comes as slightly counterintuitive if pitted against our quantitative measure of *catholic\** in the 1972 presidential campaign speeches file. Indeed—and as one could observe in Figure 4.1—McGovern actually scores the highest relative frequency value for *catholic\**. The particularly low relative frequency observed for 1988 Democratic Party candidate Dukakis (Figure 4.1) is more in tune with Sullivan's description. But in fact, the reproach that Sullivan directs at McGovern does not imply low quantitative measures, only qualitative clumsiness. In turn, such distance between quantitative measures and qualitative interpretations constitutes a strong cautionary note against those who are a bit too quick to draw Eureka conclusions from mere quantitative ebbs and flows. If anything, Sullivan's account provides highly important contextual information that needs to be considered before definite conclusions can be drawn as regards a Democratic-Party-leaning Catholic gap. As for McGovern's rhetoric proper, Sullivan's findings and our own constitute another invitation to dig deeper in the future in order to bridge this quantitative-qualitative gap.

9. To be entirely fair, it must be added that Arkedis is a senior fellow at the Progressive Policy Institute. Reading the "about" page of the Progressive Policy Institute's website (www.progressivepolicy.org/about/ Last consulted: April 12, 2018) clearly shows connections with the Democratic Party, which in turn means that Arkedis probably does not fully qualify as the average Catholic voter.

10. Opting for such reference corpora might introduce several biases—notably related to anachronism—but was still perceived as a valid approach to easily extract some of the key concepts that the Bible contains.

11. Keyness values (LL score) when tested against the OANC: *brethren* LL 3,084.91, *brother* LL 725.65, *brother's* LL 79.25; when tested against the BNC: *brethren* LL 4,573.71, *brother* LL 633.16, *brother's* LL 59.14.

12. Consider first this excerpt from Winthrop's 1630 Sermon: "[W]e must be knit together, in this work, as one man. We must entertain each other in brotherly

affection. . . . We must delight in each other; make others' conditions our own; rejoice together, mourn together, labor and suffer together, always having before our eyes our commission and community in the work, as members of the same body." The second excerpt is from the Book of Romans. The similarities with Winthrop's speech seem to suggest that Winthrop drew his inspiration from this biblical passage: "45:012:004 For as we have many members in one body, and all members have not the same office: 45:012:005 So we, being many, are one body in Christ, and every one members one of another. 45:012:010 Be kindly affectioned one to another with brotherly love; in honour preferring one another; 45:012:015 Rejoice with them that do rejoice, and weep with them that weep."

13. Interestingly, a visit (March 2014) to the White House Website revealed that Obama brought the "brother's keeper" line with him to the White House, and this to serve a program—called "My Brother's Keeper"—that aimed to address quite specific racial, communitarian and apparently all-male-oriented concerns.

14. A few remarks on Table 4.4: in the 1952 Democratic Party campaign speeches file, *commandments* has a religious meaning in every single concordance line; digging deeper into the source text confirms that 1964 Democratic Party candidate Johnson used *cheek, thee, thy, thyself* and *unto* in a religious sense; in the 1980 Democratic Party campaign speeches file, *commandment* has a religious meaning in every single concordance line.

15. On a few occasions, it was very difficult to decide whether a candidate producing a 7-word-long sequence actually used it as a Bible-inspired phrase, or else produced a string of words that coincidentally happens to be present in the Bible as well. Given that some scholars say that Biblical quotes are "integrated seamlessly and stealthily into the flow of ideas" in political speeches (Berlinerblau 2008: 84), a few passages which might not be intentionally drawn from the Bible were integrated into Table 4.7 nonetheless and tagged with the /?/ symbol in case such passages would be of said "stealth" sort. By contrast, all the passages that are not tagged with the /?/ symbol—which means almost all the passages contained in Table 4.7—were considered as clear and unmistakable quotes from the Bible.

# References

Arkedis, J. 2012. Reaching Catholics. *The New York Times' Opinion Pages*, May 18. http://campaignstops.blogs.nytimes.com/2012/05/18/reaching-catholics/?_php=true&_type=blogs&_php=true&_type=blogs&_r=2 Last consulted: September 29, 2018.

Bass, H. F. and Rozell, M. J. 2009. Religion and The U.S. Presidency. In Smidt, C.E., Kellstedt, L. A. and Guth, J. L. (eds.). *The Oxford Handbook of Religion and American Politics*. New York: Oxford University Press, 475–496.

Beasley, V. B. 2004. *You, the People: American National Identity in Presidential Rhetoric*. College Station, TX: Texas A&M University Press.

Berlinerblau, J. 2008. *Thumpin' It: The Use and Abuse of the Bible in Today's Presidential Politics*. Louisville, KY: Westminster John Knox Press.

Church, F. 2007. *So Help Me God: The Founding Fathers and the First Great Battle Over Church and State*. Orlando, FL: Harcourt, Inc.

Clermont, B. 2009. *The Neo-Catholics: Implementing Christian Nationalism in America*. Atlanta, GA: Clarity Press, Inc.

Domke, D. and Coe, K. 2008. *The God Strategy: How Religion Became a Political Weapon in America.* New York: Oxford University Press.

Edsall, T. B. 2006. *Building Red America: The New Conservative Coalition and the Drive for Permanent Power.* New York: Basic Books.

Gentile, E. 2008. *God's Democracy: American Religion After September 11,* trans. Pudney, J. and Jaus, S. D. Wesport, CT: Praeger Publishers.

Granger, S. and Paquot, M. 2010. *Statistics for Corpus Linguistics: An Introduction.* Handout, seminar in Corpus Linguistics, GERM 2825, Université Catholique de Louvain.

Gray, M. M., Perl, P. M. and Bendyna, M. E. 2006. Camelot Only Comes but Once? John F. Kerry and the Catholic Vote. *Presidential Studies Quarterly,* Vol. 36, No. 2, 2004 Presidential Election (June), 203–222.

Hunston, S. 2002. *Corpora in Applied Linguistics.* Cambridge: Cambridge University Press.

Hymnary.*org.* Website. https://hymnary.org/ Last consulted: October 15, 2018.

Mockabee, S. T., Wald, K. D. and Leege, D. C. 2009. *Is There a Religious Left? Evidence from the 2006 and 2008 ANES.* Paper prepared for the annual meeting of the American Political Science Association, Toronto, September 3–6.

O'Connell, D. 2012. *God Wills It: Presidents and the Political Use of Religion.* PhD dissertation submitted in partial fulfillment of the requirements for the degree of Doctor of Philosophy in the Graduate School of Arts and Sciences, Columbia University.

Olsen, T. 2004. Bush's Code Cracked. *Christianity Today.* www.christianitytoday. com/ct/2004/septemberweb-only/9-20-42.0.html Last consulted: September 29, 2018.

Prothero, S. 2007. *Religious Literacy: What Every American Needs to Know—And Doesn't.* New York: HarperOne.

Smith, G. S. 2006. *Faith & the Presidency: From George Washington to George W. Bush.* New York: Oxford University Press.

Steinfel, P. 2007. Roman Catholics and American Politics, 1960–2004. In Noll, M. A. and Harlow, L. E. (eds.). *Religion and American Politics: From the Colonial Period to the Present* (2nd edition). New York: Oxford University Press, 345–366.

Streb, M. J. and Frederick, B. 2008. The Myth of a Distinct Catholic Vote. In Kristin, H., Mark, J. R. and Michael A. G. (eds.). *Catholics and Politics: The Dynamic Tensions Between Faith and Power.* Washington, DC: Georgetown University Press, 93–112.

Sullivan, A. 2008. *The Party Faithful: How and Why Democrats Are Closing the God Gap.* New York: Scribner.

Teten, R. 2003. Evolution of the Modern Rhetorical Presidency: Presidential Presentation and Development of the State of the Union Address. *Presidential Studies Quarterly,* Vol. 33, No. 2 (June), 333–346.

The Pew Forum on Religion & Public Life. 2010. *U.S. Religious Knowledge Survey.* www.pewforum.org/files/2010/09/religious-knowledge-full-report.pdf Last consulted: May 23, 2014.

Vincent, A. 2014. *A Corpus Linguistics Approach to the Rhetorical God Gap in U.S. Presidential Campaigns.* Unpublished PhD thesis. Louvain-la-Neuve: Centre for English Corpus Linguistics, Université Catholique de Louvain.

Wilcox, C. and Fortelny, G. 2009. Religion and Social Movements. In Smidt, C. E., Kellstedt, L. A. and Guth, J. L. (eds.). *The Oxford Handbook of Religion and American Politics*. New York: Oxford University Press, 266–298.

Wilson, J. M. 2007. The Changing Catholic Voter: Comparing Responses to John Kennedy in 1960 and John Kerry in 2004. In Campbell, D. E. (ed.). *A Matter of Faith: Religion in the 2004 Presidential Election*. Washington, DC: Brookings Institution Press, 163–179.

# 5    Conclusion

The present book has been written with several objectives in mind. The first has been to present evidence-based findings regarding the confluence of politics and religion in presidential campaign discourse and test the hypothesis of a rhetorical God gap between a religious-sounding Republican Party and a religiously voiceless Democratic Party. Another goal has been to demonstrate that a bottom-up data-driven approach—complemented with other types of analyses—can help overcome some of the shortcomings and limitations of more traditional discourse analysis methods. Not only has our approach offered a much-needed alternative to these methods, but it has also proven to be highly versatile as it has led to some unexpected discoveries, taken us into uncharted waters, triggered quantitative and qualitative investigations into corpus data and ultimately helped confirm, question, redefine or refute several tenets of the conventional wisdom on the rhetorical God gap. Showing what effective and transferable methods and tools from corpus linguistics can bring to other branches and disciplines—be they within the American studies, rhetorical studies or discourse studies traditions—has been another important objective of the present book.

In this research, we have undertaken a corpus linguistic exploration of one facet of a long-lived, multi-faceted and—to date—still partially unknown phenomenon, to wit, the American-style relationship between religion and politics. Among the many facets of this intricate relationship, we have chosen to focus on the "rhetorical God gap" in presidential campaign rhetoric. The term "rhetorical God gap" is a direct reference to the literature from which our research question derives, as well as a reference to the conventional wisdom this study was meant to address. Although it does perfect justice to the origins of our research question, the term "rhetorical God gap" turns out to be unfair to the actual outcomes of the present research. Our data-driven approach was devised in such a way as to do more than study what a traditional understanding of the term "gap" implies, i.e. cut-and-dried differences between parties or between neatly separated eras. More precisely, by putting every candidate on equal footing and comparing each of them against the same reference corpus of general English, our analysis has actually helped reveal differences as well as similarities across time and party lines. Through a combination of quantitative, qualitative, macroscopic, microscopic, diachronic and synchronic analyses, this study has unearthed a variety of patterns of religiously laden language, be they party-specific, time-specific or else candidate-specific. As it has distanced itself from the case-study tradition and has made it possible to extract and analyze data along a broader spectrum, our approach has provided an answer to the call made for new approaches to go beyond isolated cases, undertake more encompassing studies and ultimately present findings that can help better understand how religious language has evolved in American politics both in time and across party lines.

In the present book, we have highlighted three main trends that characterize the evolution of religious-political language. The first trend concerns the early-Cold-War-specific religious language that both parties employed to express a shared anti-communist message. This historical perspective teaches some crucial lessons. Not only does it give evidence for some shared features of religious language between the GOP and the Democratic Party, but it also reminds us of the fact that the marriage between religion and politics is certainly not of recent vintage. Likewise, it puts into perspective the critique—good or bad, fair or unfair—levelled at the more recent usages of religion in politics. This is not to say that one should not keep a wary eye and critical mind towards the usage of religion for political purposes, but one should first consider the lessons from the past before calling any observed trend unprecedented, extraordinary or unacceptable. The strong biblical references that both parties exploited during the early Cold War to articulate a common worldview opposing the free world led by America to the evil godless Communist regime should serve as a benchmark—although not the only one—against which to test the more recent employment of religious-political language. More generally speaking, the Cold War deserves more consideration and more research as its impact on the role endorsed by religion in America is deep yet too often ignored.

The second trend that we have highlighted to account for the evolution of religious language in politics concerns the way the GOP has, from the late-1970s/early-1980s onwards, tapped into issues that are dear to the religious right and defended a conservative worldview—informed by the culture wars and a conservative understanding of religion—against the domestic threat of liberalism. The conservative/liberal divide on which the GOP has been so willing to insist is all the more interesting as it has been shown to align with a new framework used by scholars to describe the religious landscape in America. According to this recent framework, a conservative way of religion now opposes a more liberal religious experience and this difference is said to matter as much as, if not more than, the religious denomination one belongs to. By waging a rhetorical war against "the liberals" and depicting them as anti-religious people on the wrong side of the culture war, the GOP has tapped—willingly or not—into the new contours of the American religious landscape. It remains to be seen whether the culture-war-informed anti-liberal language that characterizes more than two decades of Republican rhetoric will stand the test of time or whether future GOP candidates will take a new rhetorical turn. Our cursory investigations into a 2016 primary debates corpus returned mixed signals as they seemed to suggest that anti-liberal rhetoric is still part of the GOP's rhetorical arsenal, yet is potentially less frequent or even absent in the rhetoric of the new—and now leading—figures of the Party. However, the 2016 primary campaign corpus is clearly limited and does not permit any kind of definite conclusions. More research on larger and more representative corpora would certainly allow a better vision into the evolution of the post-2008 campaign rhetoric for both parties. Also, only time and future research will tell us whether Donald Trump's rhetoric constitutes a true singularity when compared to that of his predecessors, running mates and successors or if it represents the first signs of a new turn in the Republican Party's political language.

Finally, our data-driven approach has returned clear signs that—contrary to conventional wisdom—the Democratic Party has produced its own religiously laden rhetorical signature. Highlighting several specific features of the Democratic-Party's religious language has been the third step of our descriptive tour of the religious rhetoric used in U.S. presidential campaigns. One of the most important lessons from that last step is that it is conceptually easy yet wrong to depict the Democratic Party as religiously voiceless. If there is indeed corpus evidence supporting the existence of differences and "gaps" between the GOP and the Democratic Party's rhetoric, these differences are nonetheless of another and more complex nature than those found in the commonly adopted polarity between a religious GOP and a godless Democratic Party. Unlike the GOP though, it is not on the culture-war front that one will find the most paradigmatic examples of the Democratic Party's religious rhetoric. Indeed, we have shown that several Democratic Party candidates tried to fight back and address the culture-war-related stances of their opponents without necessarily achieving the desired outcome. Parenthetically, but importantly, the discrepancy that has been observed between—on the one hand—the relatively equal quantitative measures of references to *family values* produced by both parties and—on the other hand—the general agreement that the GOP still "owns" the family-value issue clearly calls for future investigations into issue ownership theories. In spite of the resistance shown by certain Democratic Party leaders, one has to conclude that the Democratic Party has lost some ground on the culture-war rhetorical front, and has tacitly abandoned the term *liberal* to their opponents. Only in that respect does it seem broadly correct to depict the Democratic Party's religious rhetoric mostly as a response to the GOP's rhetoric of culture wars and anti-liberalism. However, one should not mistake one feature of the Democratic Party's rhetoric for the ensemble and conclude that it has not produced its own brand of religious language. As documented in the last chapter of the present book, the Democratic Party's religious rhetoric has notably been characterized by its insistence on specific religious denominations, suggesting that—willingly or not—the Democratic Party candidates still draw from the "religious belonging" framework used to depict a more traditional understanding of the religious landscape in America. In our study, we have concentrated on a brief analysis of the references to Catholics and left aside the other references to religious denominations that our analyses had detected. In turn, we called for future research efforts into the detection and analyses of direct and indirect references to specific religious denominations. We reiterate the very same call here. Whereas the GOP's campaign rhetoric has been marked by issues held dear by the religious right, we have also shown that the language produced by the Democratic Party has been marked by a religiously loaded—and sometimes biblically inspired—vision of solidarity and mutual responsibility that probably resonates quite strongly with the religious left. So far, the links between the GOP and the religious right have drawn most of the attention of pundits and scholars alike, so it seems quite important in the future to start restoring the balance somehow and devote more research to the religious left. Finally, we have presented a totally unexpected discovery in the form of biblical language—sometimes quoted verbatim from the Bible—and shown that it constitutes a distinctive feature of Democratic campaign speeches. However, nothing has been said yet on the purposes that such language could serve, and more qualitative investigations into the messages conveyed through this biblical language would certainly be a welcome addition to the present study. Likewise, we have put to the test some beliefs and claims on the presence of the Bible in political language, but the extent to which other forms of biblical language have potentially made their way into the rhetorical arsenal of politicians is not clear yet and should be further investigated. Developing new methods to detect and analyze "in-stealth-mode" religious rhetoric—claimed to be real by many scholars and pundits alike—seems to be one of the first steps to take next. We have also called for more attention to be paid to some paradoxical findings, notably regarding the widespread religious illiteracy of the American people that makes it quite hard to believe that hidden or less obvious religious messages are heard and, even less so, deciphered. Whatever the methodological path taken in the future, it is urgent to recognize once and for all the need to substantiate claims with solid evidence and to test the quality of that evidence and the methods employed to elicit it.

All in all, the picture returned in this study is that of a patchwork made of different types of political-religious language. Although still incomplete, there is no doubting the fact that the picture returned by our study is not as simplistic as the one suggested by the premise that this research has sought to address, and which narrowly depicts a fairly recent rhetorical gap separating an all-religious GOP from a religiously voiceless Democratic Party. One of the conclusions we can certainly draw from this study is therefore that of a picture which is far more complex than the black and white version still pervading much of the conventional understanding of religion and politics in America. Such a version is surely easier to understand and probably easier to sell too, but it is misleading and wrong.

# Index

Note: numbers in **bold** indicate a table; numbers in *italics* indicate a figure.

72; use of *culture of life* 80, 88; war on terror 5, 26
Brezina, V. 65, 67

campaign ads *see* presidential campaign ads
campaign debates *see* presidential campaign debates
campaign rhetoric *see* presidential campaign rhetoric
campaign speeches see presidential campaign speeches
Carter, Jimmy **11**, 32n9, 50, 51, 59, 61–64, 110
*catholic* (keyword) 6, 87; *see also* Catholics
*catholic\** (query) *88, 91, 92*
Catholic Daughters of America 90
"Catholic gap" 80
Catholic Golden Age 90
Catholic pattern 38, 86–96
Catholics 43; Clinton's position toward 95; and individualist/communitarian divide 94; Kennedy as 91–92; and the religious left 99–100, 103; and sisterhood 103; support for Republican Party 89–90; *see also* Protestant-Catholic-Jewish
Christian conservatives 36, 45; and judicial grievances 58; *see also* Christian Right; conservatives; evangelical Christians
Christian Hymn corpus 3, 15, 107, 117–118, **118**
Christian Left 117
Christian Right 42, 44–45, 117; and Falwell 64; and "family values" 40, 49–51; and same-sex marriage 56
Christianity 29, 122
Clinton, Hillary 103–104
Clinton, William (Bill) **11**, 28–29, 50, 51, 54, 55, **72**; Bible-citing 106–107, 113; *brotherhood*, views on 101–102; *Catholics*, position on 90–97; fetal tissue research 41–43; liberal/conservative divide 75–76
Coe, K. 2, 15, 17, 26, 36; on family values 43–46, 49, 51; on the "God Strategy" 89–90; on judicial activism 57–61; morality politics strategy 37; on stem cell research 40

Cold War 4–5; early Cold War 20–31; *crusade* references during 28–29; ideological warfare against Communism 30; U.S. presidents during 25
collocation 61; analyses 3, 14, 21, 65, 67; frequency 66; network 65, 66, *68, 69*; patterns 59
collocation network around the node *conservative\** in the 2016 GOP primary debates subcorpus *69*
collocation network around the node *liberal\** in the 2016 GOP primary debates subcorpus **66**, *68*
Collocation Parameters Notation (CPN) 65
collocation patterns for the nodes *judges/judicial/justices* in the 1972, 1988, 1996, 2004 and 2008 GOP campaign speeches files *60*
Communism 4–5, 20–25, 29–31, 80, 128
*Concord* tool 24, 113–114
concordance 3, 14, 21, 70; on abortion 39; on *atheis\* 25*; on the Bible 109–110, 114; on *brethren* 102; on *brotherhood* 103; *catholic\** 92, *92*; on *conservative\** 68; on *crusade\** 28; on *evil\** 29; on *family value\** 46, *47, 49*, 51; on *judges* 59–60, *61*, 64; on *liberal\** 76; on *marriage* 54; on pro-life 41; on *sisterhood* 103; on *socialism* 98; on *unborn* 37
Concordance lines from query *activistjud\*/judicialactivis\** in the 1952–2008 Presidential Campaign Speeches corpus *61*
concordance lines for query *atheis\*/ godless/nonbeliev\*/non believ\* 25*
concordance lines from the Bible-specific 7-gram search list in the PCS Corpus *114*
concordance lines returned from the query *catholic\** in the 1992 Democratic Party campaign speeches file *92*
concordance lines for the two-word query *family value\** in the Democratic Party campaign speeches files *47*

134    *Index*

For Product Safety Concerns and Information please contact our EU
representative GPSR@taylorandfrancis.com
Taylor & Francis Verlag GmbH, Kaufingerstraße 24, 80331 München, Germany

www.ingramcontent.com/pod-product-compliance
Lightning Source LLC
Chambersburg PA
CBHW050529270326
41926CB00015B/3141

9 780367 787783